Patrolling
Cyberspace

Lessons Learned from a
Lifetime in Data Security

By Howard A. Schmidt

Foreword by Governor Tom Ridge—First Secretary of Homeland Security

Patrolling Cyberspace
Lessons Learned from a Lifetime in Data Security
By Howard A. Schmidt — Former FBI Computer Specialist, CSO Microsoft, CSO eBay, White House CyberSecurity Advisor

Published by Larstan Publishing, Inc., 10604 Outpost Dr., N. Potomac MD, 20878, 240-396-0007, ext. 901, www.larstan.com

PRINTED IN THE UNITED STATES OF AMERICA

10 9 8 7 6 5 4 3 2 1

Design by Mike Gibson/Love Has No Logic Design Group (lovehasnologic.com)

ISBN, Print Edition 978-0-9776895-2-1

Library of Congress Control Number: 2006938062

First Edition

To my loving wife, Raemarie, and our four boys,
Kyle, Anthony, David and Andrew,
who make us proud in everything they do

ACKNOWLEDGEMENTS

I am grateful to the friends and colleagues who took time out of their busy lives to help shape the events depicted in this book, including Danny Mares, Mike Gibbons, Mike Anderson, Scott Charney, Bruce Burbridge, Dale Drew, Andrew Fried and Christopher Stippich.

Also, this book is very much a team effort, and it would not have been possible were it not for the folks at Larstan Publishing, people like Eric Green, David Evancha, Shawna McAlearney, Mike Gibson and Anne Saita.

In addition, sentences were smoothed out and facts verified thanks to the assistance of William Ferguson, manager of corporate partnerships for Carnegie Mellon University's CyLab; Citlalli Solano-Leonce and Mario R. Rincón, both at Carnegie Mellon University's Information Networking Institute; Amit S. Tambe at the Georgia Institute of Technology; and Amin Y. Teymorian at George Washington University.

Finally, there's Raemarie, my wife and my muse, who did a great job checking over my work.

TABLE OF CONTENTS

FOREWORD By Gov. Tom Ridge **9**

ONE Political Protest or Criminal Intent? **13**

TWO Adversity as a Mother of Invention **43**

THREE Worming a Way into History **65**

FOUR Fighting 21st Century Crime with 18th Century Laws **83**

FIVE From Fame to Fortune **103**

SIX An International Affair **123**

SEVEN Safeguarding Our Goods **143**

EIGHT Where We're Most Vulnerable **159**

NINE The Highway Ahead **179**

FOREWORD

– Governor Tom Ridge
First Secretary, U.S. Department of Homeland Security

Government has long sought to protect people and places from the threats of those wanting to do harm. Those protections come in many forms, from physical safety features within brick-and-mortar buildings to newer intrusion detection devices installed on domestic and global telecommunications networks.

In the 21st century, the physical and cyber environments are far from exclusive domains; rather, the two have become closely intertwined, meaning attempts to sabotage one can have equally dire consequences for the other. Virus writers, for example, can exploit flawed systems to corrupt and cripple computer data. Consider the impact that could have on an electric grid that provides life-sustaining power to millions of homes, hospitals and other businesses. Those grids today are part of a vast technological backbone, such that a few lines of well-placed code could put our citizens, our businesses and our nation at great risk.

These are new times. While hacking used to be the pastime of the ego-driven who infiltrated networks just to prove that they could, today we have enemies who reside within terror cells, organized crime and unstable regions throughout the world. They endeavor to use our telecommunications systems as a means to do us harm. This requires a much greater awareness of the vulnerabilities that exist today and a heightened need for responsible citizens to help secure the portions of cyberspace that they own, operate and control.

We all have a role to play in hardening our nation against cyber-attacks—one that we need to take more seriously. The Internet provides universal access to data, and while it was designed for the best and most positive of uses, its ubiquity also makes it useful to people with malevolent intentions.

That's why this book, *Patrolling Cyberspace*, is important and instructive. Using layman's language instead of technical jargon, readers will come to understand why the need for better products and security-mindful users is vital to our future, and why each facet of our society plays a key role in improving protections.

The industry that produces the hardware and software running mission-critical systems has become far more sensitive to the role its products play in attacks. We applaud that effort and yet we must ask them to do more. Security must be embedded throughout our cyber programs and devices. It must be rigorously tested earlier and more frequently during development to makes sure products are immune to attack.

Additionally, Internet consumers have a responsibility to take precautions to detect and deter intrusions. Otherwise, their unprotected PCs will continue to aid the criminal element through the spread of debilitating viruses, Trojan horses and worms designed to steal identities and financial data later used to fund organized crime and terrorist activities.

As a nation, we are still grappling with the role government should take to increase corporate and citizen responsibility. Will it be through regulation? A litany of government mandates? Nudging the research and development community into stronger action? Or does a combination of these actions provide the solution? It may be too soon to know.

However, Howard Schmidt's book helps guide us toward a solution. In the following pages, he describes the Internet, in all its glory and vulnerability. He takes us through the evolution of cybercrime and the growing sophistication of those who use this global communications tool as a tool for terror, destruction, fraud and deceit.

Based upon a lifetime of experience in this field, Howard is able to show that, much like technology itself, the sophistication and complexity needed to apprehend cybercriminals has grown exponentially. That's a strong and powerful message for anyone who depends and relies on the constructive use of the Internet. In a changing world, it's a message of vital importance to us all.

CHAPTER ONE

Political Protest or Criminal Intent?

"The Bell system is the biggest ripoff monopoly in the world. It charges exorbitant, ever-increasing rates, and collects taxes for the war machine. It is the only Kompany [sic] allowed to send up satelites [sic] via government rockets; private corporations were denied the right to compete and thereby infringe on Bell's exclusive rights to overseas call revenues."

Opening lines of a Youth International Party Line flyer released May 1, 1971, in Washington, D.C.

Today, the term "hacker" often conveys a picture of a brilliant, if twisted, criminal out to steal. Doesn't matter about the object of theft–credit cards, identities, government secrets, corporate projects–these are essentially people doing obviously bad things. But that hasn't always been the case. Indeed, there was a time when being known as a hacker held a certain level of respect, if within limited circles. And let's not confuse the word with "phreaker," which we'll discuss later. The term initially referred to someone who could get the most out of the somewhat primitive software that accompanied the first several generations of mainframes that dominated the information technology landscape in the 1960s and 1970s.

I remember the first time I was briefed on a case involving John Draper, upon whom much has been written. Having been a HAM radio operator for a number of years, I was familiar with the concept of creating touch tone signals to switch radio equipment and dial-in telephone systems, etc., and found it particularly interesting that this was being used for criminal activity. The Bay Area man once bragged of placing international calls for free by exploiting vulnerabilities in the phone company's routing systems and faulty equipment that could be manipulated. It's important to note that back in the day, pay phones were quite popular for those needing to place a call "on the run," unlike today's cell phones, which have made the telephone booth increasingly obsolete.

Notwithstanding the fact his acts constituted theft of services, Draper has long maintained that he wasn't interested in getting free long distance but in understanding how this ubiquitous system worked and how he could personally manipulate it. Since the phone company could track activity on private lines, public pay phones became a beacon for nefarious expeditions done to assuage curiosity. One of Draper's favorite activities was to find two public phones located next to each other. He would then "phreak" one phone into routing a call from California across the country, linking to communications satellites and international systems until the call came back and rung on the pay telephone next to the one he was using. The lag time within this labyrinth of connections allowed him to have a conversation with himself that literally went around the world. He'd also make calls to international locations just to ask about weather. In fact, Draper was so adept at hacking, that he could do things with the phone system that even the phone system couldn't do.

Of all his antics, though, the one he is most closely associated with involved the work of blind hackers. They discovered if you sealed the third hole in a cereal's promotional toy whistle it emulated one of the two tones that's generated when you press a specific key on a touch-tone phone key pad, known as dual-tone multi-frequency. By covering the hole, the tone generated imitated the trunk code that allowed long distance transmission. Another plastic whistle made to look like an Oscar Meyer weiner did the same thing for the other frequency.

Draper was indeed viewed as a hot dog among the nascent community of hackers, a network of kids, college students and electronics enthusiasts who wanted to see just how far their curiosity and computing expertise would take them. This new group of people exploiting telephone systems became known as "phreakers." With the plastic whistle Draper and the others created a scam that not only helped usher in a new era of high-tech crime but solidified Draper's reputation as ring leader among arguably the most influential and colorful network of hackers.

His tricks would ramp up, and his reach would widen. Draper would pay homage to that cereal that in some ways catapulted him to infamy. Thus, when it came time to switch his online identity from just John to something far more interesting, he decided on the alias Cap'n Crunch.

In recent years, the telecommunications evolution in the United States appears to have paralleled that of information processing. But up until deregulation in the 1980s, the phone company was, except for some basically meaningless competition, a monopoly. Ma Bell, as it was nationally known, owned the local calls, the long distance lines and even the telephones themselves. The phone company could charge pretty much what it wanted and provide whatever level of service it deemed satisfactory. Between its monopolistic attitudes to its large, complex network, the lure to pull one over on the telecommunications industry was irresistible to a number of misguided and obsessed individuals.

In several important ways, it was by the direct action of the phone company during the mid to late 1950s that the keys to its system unofficially were offered to these willing takers. At that time, the phone company decided to replace its legion of operators with a computerized, direct-dial system that used musical notes, or multi-frequency tones, to dial and route calls to a specific number. This was Ma Bell's first flaw, but one curious computer enthusiasts might have been willing to overlook. What they couldn't ignore was what was seen by many at the time as an act of arrogance that only a monopoly, secure in its position, would commit–it published the electronic signals that it used for routing long distance and for billing in two issues of its *Bell System Technical Journal*. This journal, written for Bell System engineers, was also part of the subscription library at most engineering colleges of the day. Bell belatedly tried to recall these two issues, but not before these codes were copied and passed along to engineering students across the country. Once the tone system was known, it was simple for engineering students and others to reproduce them. Hence, in an unintended and important way, the phone company itself provided the information which led to the creation of the first generation of phone phreakers.

With the genie out of the bottle, beating the phone company became the obsession of anyone with criminal intent and the ability to do so. Notwithstanding it amounted to the theft of phone service, and thus was a criminal act. But this was so attractive that otherwise law-abiding families and individuals had devised their own ways to get around hefty service charges and fees. Anyone could lick a penny to "bounce" a pay phone for a free call or use code words during a person-to-person hook up to transfer a message without paying for long distance. Such practices were pervasive and void of malicious intent.

But many of these original phreakers actually maintained a love-hate relationship with the phone company; it might have charged too much, but at the same it allowed them to do things they couldn't before. The group Draper was introduced to was led by blind hackers who delighted that sight was not required for success. They were mesmerized by the size and complexity of the phone network, its technology and communications tools. It was the noncompetitive price for service and equipment that they and just about everyone hated. The phone company's monopoly made it an unsympathetic victim, although it was still a victim. "Phreaking" it out of a few bucks was not generally viewed as a high crime. But that would change.

The engineering students with this tonal Rosetta Stone immediately began working on the best way to repeat perfectly the sounds asked for by the phone system on demand. These efforts initially took the form of boxes that were about the size of the telephone and were named for their color. For example, there were red boxes that many engineering students used to talk with distant parents for free, and black boxes most often used by bookies for the same purpose–sans parents. The most sophisticated and eventually most widely used device was the blue box. This box actually put its users in direct control of the long distance switching equipment. In a series of related episodes of unintended consequences, it was this blue box that both created the opportunity for the technological leap that facilitated computer hacking and introduced the benefits of phreaking. It also created the crevasse in which the seriously criminal element did enter. All of this was accomplished well within seven degrees of separation.

The Blue Box, Cap'n Crunch and Prison Survival

Though John Draper, a.k.a. Cap'n Crunch, adopted his *nom de hacker* from a cereal of that name, he wasn't a big user of the device. His real focus rested in his ability to manipulate the phone system using a blue box.

The conundrum the legal community now faced, and would for years to come, was how to classify this new breed of technology criminal. But in Draper's case, 18th-century laws on theft of services actually applied, even if the current legal configuration could never have been imagined by our forefathers. He was convicted of stealing and sent to prison.

Putting someone positioned as a "computer hobbyist"—someone we'd refer to today as a geek—into prison with more hardened criminals doing time for violent crimes or property theft certainly put the Cap'n in a position he'd never been in before—and hopefully wouldn't face again. Needing to survive in this hostile and dangerous place, Draper allegedly made a deal with a cell block power lord to trade his extensive knowledge of the phone system for protection. In this way, much of the knowledge of one of the most experienced phone phreakers entered into the criminal underworld.

Berkeley Blue, Oak Toebark and the Personal Computer

Right before his arrest in 1972, Draper attended a meeting of the People's Computer Company in Menlo Park, Calif. The purpose of this "company" was to learn how computers worked, basically by dismantling a Digital Equipment Corporation minicomputer. As interest in the concept of a "personal computer" grew, some members of this group joined together a few years later to form the Homebrew Computer Club in 1975. That same year, the first personal computer, the Altair 8800, went on the market in kit form. The Homebrew Club was now motivated to develop its own PC.

Two members of this club were already making and selling blue boxes on a quantity basis. To maintain a degree of anonymity, they assumed the aliases of Berkeley Blue and Oak Toebark. At that time, manufacturing and selling blue boxes was legal; although using them was not. The two made and sold hundreds of these electronic devices before Oak Toebark expressed interest in owning one of these new personal computers. However, he didn't have the cash to buy one so he designed and built his own. This design proved superior to existing systems and Oak Toebark, a.k.a. Steve Wozniak, and Berkeley Blue, a.k.a. Steve Jobs, were able to leverage their acumen in building blue boxes to build Apple Computers.

Not that anyone would expect it, but the small world of phone phreakers became central to the development of the PC, which,

What's A Blue Box?

A blue box was a phreaking tool that mimicked a telephone operator's dialing console. The device duplicated the tones used to switch long-distance calls, thereby bypassing the usual mechanisms to route a call and allowing the caller to talk long-distance for free.

of course, became the core tool for ever more and greater feats of computer hacking. Without being overly nostalgic, the early days of phone phreaking very much reflected the antiestablishment movements of the late 1960s and early 1970s. Stealing free long distance could be rationalized as liberation from an overbearing monopoly.

Every society has its hierarchy, and the bottom feeders of telecommunications thieves during this time period were the "carders." These people took advantage of phone card codes, then the new long-distance access technology. One of the many types of cards was the "FONCARD" offered by Sprint that provided access to long distance lines, which was especially useful for calls made while traveling. Carders would hang around big city airports like LAX, LaGuardia, O'Hare and Kennedy and conduct an exercise called "shoulder surfing." A carder would first wait for a potential victim to approach a bank of public phone machines. He then would stand next to the victim and fake like he was talking while, in reality, he was looking over the victim's shoulder and writing down the calling card or credit card number the victim used.

Another carding technique was to sit off in the background and watch where a target's fingers hit on the keys, write the number down on a slip of paper and, almost like a bookie, hand the number off to a runner. The runner would deliver these numbers to a co-conspirator in the vicinity, who'd take it outside the airport and pass it off to a seller. It was not uncommon to then find people lined up at a street corner telephone booth within the next half hour making international calls using that pilfered calling card information. At the same time, these secret codes were posted on electronic bulletin boards where people throughout the country could access and abuse them. This low-tech thievery was brought to new levels by phreakers using PC technology and modems.

The Last Days of Disco & The Rise of Bulletin Boards

Just as disco, the pop culture phenomenon that came to define the 70s, was on its last breath, the first viable and actually useful personal computer bulletin board was born. The year was 1978.

The development of the PC was as much a social event as a technological one, bringing computing power down from what many viewed as the "capitalist corporations" to the everyday people. The fact that the personal computer would spawn its own monopoly, with several large corporations providing the lion's share of software on which they ran, is an ironic conse-quence. What mattered then was that a fully assembled, capa-ble personal computer system was now available to the masses. Combined with a modem, a new breed of phreaker/hacker was now empowered with even more power and freedom. From this convergence of technology emerged the era of bulletin board systems.

A bulletin board system was easy to create. As an avid HAM radio operator and electronics enthusiast, I became interested in these newly accessible computers and ran a couple of bulletin boards myself using my Commodore 64 or Sanyo CPM machine connected to a phone line through an external modem. Another user, deploying one of three different types of freely available software would dial a regular phone number such as 602-123-4567 in Arizona, that would connect to the bulletin board and be welcomed with a login screen at whatever modem speed the caller had (from 300 baud or 2400 baud, as were available then). The screen would then broadcast: "Welcome to Howard's BBS."

There were many options to these salutations available to the skilled systems operator (sysop) who ran these boards. From this entry screen, callers gave their user ID and password. Upon entry, users would have access to everything from file sharing to "freeware" and "shareware" exchanges. As with most computer-related activities, bulletin boards began as hobbies of the technological elite skilled at using what by today's standards we'd consider primitive technology. They were not averse to writing enabling software themselves. However, as the technology became simpler to use, the number of U.S.-based bulletin boards blossomed from some 4,000 in 1985 to more than 30,000 in 1990. Most of these boards were harmless mediums used to exchange free software and to share information, even to enable electronic transfer of messages and documents. Original commercial networks like Compuserv and Prodigy were mainly quite large and complex manifestations of the bulletin board concept. Boards supported all kinds of interests, from aviation to adult pornography, from SCUBA to skydiving. Others that went deeply underground were involved in distribution of child pornography, stolen credit cards and pirated software.

When we talk about patrolling cyberspace, these bulletin boards are where many of us had our beginnings in investigating high-tech crimes. Some of the first successful criminal cases were against a child pornography ring that utilized bulletin boards to exchange information (more on this in Chapter Two). However, most of these underground boards weren't directly afoul of the law; instead, they stood squarely within gray areas. One bulletin board in St Louis operated by two phreakers known by the 'nyms (slang for pseudonyms) Knight Lightning and Taran King was dedicated to spreading gossip and information about phone phreaking and computer hacking with a distinct dash of anarchy and aggressive anti-social behavior. The two published it under the title Phrack (phreak + hack) beginning in 1985 after earlier being known as Metal Shop BBS.

Phrack was a freely downloaded electronic magazine that resonated with the hacker underground, reaching iconic status quickly. It also reached the attention of federal agents and state and local law enforcement officials suddenly wearing a new hat (if unofficially) within the force, that of the "cybercop."

As a matter of record, Phrack was silenced for several months in 1990 when its original editors/operators were arrested during Operation SunDevil, the codename for a nationwide crackdown on computer hackers. Though plenty of carders and other petty thieves were caught in the dragnet, it was the arrests of Phrack's editors for publishing a private 911 emergency response system document copied from a BellSouth computer that drew the most media attention. Phrack continued under a new editor and published periodically up to August 2005, but without instructions for making bombs and projec-

Sampling of Phrack' Contents

November 11, 1985

Making an Acetylene Balloon Bomb

Using MCI Calling Cards

Homemade Guns

Homemade Blowguns

Making Shell Bombs

March 3, 1986

Crashing DEC-10s*

False Identification—Changing a Driver's License to Make One 21 Years Old

Making Crystal Meth

April 18, 1986

Hacking DEC 10s

Hand-to-Hand Combat

Source: The Art of Hacking

* a popular minicomputer in the 1980s

tile weapons that were a staple of earlier issues. Rumors of its re-emergence have circulated since its demise.

Of course, not all bulletin board technology was engineered for questionable use. Many were created for commercial purposes. Cash was starting to be replaced by plastic credit and debit cards. To accommodate the new breed of shopper, big department stores created online database systems to support credit cards' acceptance in the absence of an information technology (IT) department. In creating such a setup, the database company might also drop in a type of bulletin board so its system technicians could troubleshoot the application by dialing it up via a modem through a dedicated maintenance phone line provided by the department store. These databases quickly came under siege by hackers.

At this point, phone phreaks were gaining access to other computer systems as well as the primitive network of university and government systems called the ARPANET, short for the Advanced Research Projects Agency Network. ARPANET was the technological predecessor to the Internet. Access to it began to create distinctions between different types of hackers. Hackers of that day always maintained they weren't criminal but merely exploring as "clever hobbyists" this vast and expanding universe of cyberspace.

There was one hacker who because of his activity irritated fellow hackers to the point where they actually banded together to aid police in tracking him down. Numerous published accounts explain that Kevin Mitnick adopted the alias Condor from the movie *Three Days of the Condor* and developed an insatiable appetite for flaunting his criminal activity in the face of law enforcement and other hackers. The Condor's reputation reached such proportions that he reportedly was placed in solitary confinement during a portion of his incarceration because prison authorities were convinced that he could disrupt network services simply by using the prison phone system.

Mitnick's infamy grew, making him at one point "America's Most Wanted Computer Outlaw." He became known more widely after he became the subject of a 1996 book *Takedown: The Pursuit and Capture of Kevin Mitnick, America's Most Wanted Computer Outlaw-By the Man Who Did It*. In the book, authors Tsutomu Shimomura and John Markoff chronicle Mitnick's misdeeds and eventual capture after hacking into Shimomura's San Diego-based computer.

Cyber Gangs and the Fine Art of War Dialing

Bulletin boards also provided a means for people with similar interests to band together and share experiences. One early one, Plovernet, operated on the East Coast and served as

> "Would you like to play a game?"
>
> **Query posed by a DoD computer controlling a U.S. nuclear arsenal to a teenaged hacker in the movie War Games**

a magnet for phone phreakers who'd crossed into hackerdom. One member of this board went by the handle of Lex Luthor. In 1984, Lex Luthor started his own BBS called the Legion of Doom. (For those of you who have never read a comic book or watched a superhero cartoon, Lex Luthor is Superman's nemesis, and the Legion of Doom was a band of arch villains with their own super powers that opposed Superman, Batman and their Justice League. The fictitious handles assumed by these early hackers revealed much: These were young people who did not view cyberspace as entirely real.) Lex Luthor's personal genius in phreaking the phone system soon attracted a number of similarly minded and gifted members into this group. The Legion of Doom, or LoD for short, quickly recruited more members with newer, and infinitely more fascinating, computer intrusion skills.

A standard technique used by both phreakers and hackers to find useful targets was a process called war dialing. The technique was first presented to the public in a 1983 movie called *War Games*, where a young man played by Matthew Broderick uses a home computer to break into the Department of Defense's computer that controls the nuclear arsenal, as well as other functions. Broderick programmed a computer to start dialing phone numbers sequentially. When the war dialer connected to a modem tone on the receiving end, that number was recorded. The hacker would then go back later and dial in from a personal computer and connect to that system's login screen. At that time, the user ID would often be "root" (representing the highest level of authority over a computer) and the password something obvious like 1234, which was the default code that manufacturers recommended be changed–a request usually ignored.

With the ID and the password, hackers like the one in *War Games* would obtain access to a system as the system's operator, also known as the sysop. At this level they would be able to copy credit card and phone card numbers, turn systems off and set up accounts. This would be a precursor to how current hackers penetrate web servers and conduct an Internet hack. By using war dialing techniques, this new brand of phreaks could use the telephone system, which they had compromised into providing free long distance calls, to bring them into contact with telephone-interfacing computer systems or to connect with the small but growing community of systems connected by networks such as the Tymnet routing service, Bitnet and, of course, ARPANET—basically every system in government, academia and the private sector.

At the same time, a plethora of "cybergangs" grew up around the bulletin boards. Most had fanciful or fearsome names like Neon Light, The Ice Pirates, Insanity Inc. and Free World II, but none had the sheer gall and self-promotion of the Legion of Doom (LoD). The LoD was established from the ruins of two earlier BBSes, the Knights of Shadow and the Tribunal of Knowledge. Even at its height, the LoD was never more than a loose confederation of individuals, many of which never met face to face and always referred to each other by their pseudonyms when conducting legion business. Central members, besides Lex Luthor, included Blue Archer, Gary Seven, Kerrang Khan, Master of Impact, Silver Spy, The Marauder, The VideoSmith and The Mentor. The infamous Phiber Optik and Acid Phreak would join later.

LoD's fame and reputation was centered on members' insatiable desire to blanket the entire digital underworld with information and knowledge gained through less-than-legal activities. They managed to appear, with regularity, on every important BBS that was or yearned to be a pirate, a board used to post and exchange hacker ideas and display "trophies." They even ran several of their own boards. Most importantly, they were mainstays in Phrack, the previously mentioned hacker magazine. These guys were skilled hackers, but they also were expert promoters and more than willing to strut and brag. With unmatched bravado, they even published a periodical that they titled *The Legion of Doom Technical Journal.* This journal was the evil twin of the phone company's technical journal and often presented the hacker's view within the articles that it published. Although this taunting and outright mockery was not illegal, it did get people's attention. The phone companies, the FBI and other government agencies became some of the journal's most avid readers.

By 1986, it appeared to those not deeply in the know that the LoD comprised the digital underground. However, the legion's membership was never really that large. There were no dues or identification cards required, so membership remained somewhat fluid. At some point in time, the LoD stopped becoming a cybergang and started becoming a metaphor for all phreakers and hackers. It had become the gang that would not die.

By 1990, the Legion of Doom was not just a group of exploring teenagers. But its reputation remained big and, by then, a whole new generation of hackers had learned their trade by reading LoD instructive manuals. Curiously, this gang's reputation up to this time was based on skill and system mastery, not on blatant criminal activity. The best hackers were less likely to have committed a crime. Obviously, they did not consider ripping off the telephone company as a crime. Legion of Doom members were indeed legends in their own time, but it was that spirit of braggadocio that eventually would bring it down.

Fry Guy and the Road to Ruin

The original cast of LoD spawned spin-off "cells" and a minion of wannabes. The next and crucial chapter of the Legion's infamy was bound in both.

> "The Legion of Doom was less a high-tech street gang than an on-going state of mind."
>
> **Bruce Sterling, author of Hacker Crackdown**

One longtime LoD member with the handle Control-C gained the attention of Michigan Bell with his ability to dominate the entire system. In 1987, this telephone company finally apprehended Control-C and found him to be a likeable and brilliant telephone fanatic. Since very little real harm was committed by Control-C, Michigan Bell decided not to press charges. On the contrary, they actually hired Control-C as a high-profile "scarecrow" focused on deterring other invaders of this phone system. This event sparked the myth that good hackers would not be prosecuted since their skill sets would be of value to those systems that they targeted. That myth would eventually and unequivocally be debunked.

As already stated, LoD was a loose organization at best. One of its "cells" based in Atlanta was led by Urvile, Prophet and Leftist, who become notorious as "owners" of the BellSouth telephone system. As was often the case with the LoD, it was the recognized ability of these three to hack BellSouth at will which earned them LoD status more than a formal initiation from LoD royalty like Lex Luthor and, by this time, Erik Bloodaxe. This particular cell's work was accomplished with such skill and elusiveness that, even when BellSouth was informed of its numerous activities, it didn't believe nor act upon it. Typical for the LoD, the Georgia contingent was not shy in broadcasting its achievements.

Especially bold in his self-aggrandizement was Urvile. He contributed to many pirate boards including the Altos chat board located in Bonn, Germany. There, Urvile traded hacking secrets for the high-end operating system known as VMS with many of his international colleagues including Jaeger and Pengo, two Hanover-based Germans belonging to the Chaos Computer Club, which later was implicated in a KGB-sponsored international spy ring detailed in Clifford Stoll's 1990 book *The Cuckoo's Egg: Tracking a Spy Through the Maze of Computer Espionage*. Also frequenting this chat board was a 16-year-old LoD wannabe and McDonald's fast food aficionado who went by the handle Fry Guy. The teen was enthralled with LoD, and the group's easy interaction with hackers Jaeger and Pengo just enhanced his attraction. So, he set out to emulate them, with one major difference: Fry Guy liked to steal.

Learning at the feet of Urvile and other LoD members via his interaction with the Altos chat board, Fry Guy became adept at both manipulating phone switches and illegally copying credit card numbers. Fry Guy's first claim to fame was in crossing the long distance switches so that calls made to the Palm Beach County Probation Department were being answered by a phone sex line in New York City. This annoying, if humorous, prank served as a wake-up call to BellSouth that there were unauthorized users of its systems.

BellSouth, along with everyone else, suspected the LoD. Fry Guy then combined the two techniques learned on the Altos board to first steal money from Western Union and then to purloin goods by mail order. His total take was approximately $6,000. Another bad habit learned from LoD was a penchant to brag about his accomplishments. Fry Guy, believing he was impervious to capture, actually called Indiana Bell to brag about his exploits directly to his victim. However, by this time, the phone companies and other government agencies had galvanized to counter computer attacks conducted by an international espionage operation known as The Cuckoo Egg. This helped authorities quickly track down Fry Guy. Authorities found a confused and blubbering teenager ready to drop a dime on anyone if it lessened the severity of his punishment. The LoD were prime targets.

Fry Guy unloaded everything he'd learned to the U.S. Secret Service, giving LoD members full credit. This, even though he was never a member of LoD, nor had he ever met a LoD member in person. No matter, this was a smoking gun and an opportunity to thoroughly investigate the three Atlanta-based LoD marauders who were taking liberties with the BellSouth system. In addition, Fry Guy told the authorities that the LoD could bring down the entire nationwide phone system at will and planned to do so on some future holiday. This later would be a major bone of contention.

The Masters of Deception: Bold, Brash, Brilliant... and Busted

Fry Guy's contrition and eagerness to claim that he was hopelessly under the spell of the LoD played a major part in the group's demise, starting with the Atlanta-based cell. But the LoD's own activities in 1988

> "We neither advocate, condone nor participate in any sort of illicit behavior. But we will sit back and watch."
> **Knight Lightning, editor of Phrack**

and 1989 provided more than enough cause for law enforcement agencies to bring down the hammer. The convergence of these activities in coincidence with other random events was a primary cause of one of the first major crackdowns on hackers in the United States.

The first event occurred in 1988 when the hacker Prophet broke into BellSouth's centralized automation system, or Advanced Information Management System (AIMSX). There, among numerous articles and documents, he found a large, somewhat esoteric manual titled *Bell South Standard Practice 660-225-104SV Control Office Administration of Enhanced 911 Services for Special Services and Major Account Centers.* Prophet did no damage to this system, but he took this impressive sounding document as a trophy. He then did what LoD members usually did: He began to show off. This document eventually came to the attention of Phrack editor Knight Lightning. The editors decided to publish an edited version of this document on what's now called an Enhanced 911(E911) service in the Phrack magazine. At the time, in February of 1989, Phrack was published internationally on 150 sites.

At about this time, two members of the LoD, The Mentor and Erik Bloodaxe began a new bulletin board called the Phoenix Project. This board had the ambitious and audacious goals of both reviving a perceived stagnating digital underground and to bring LoD and telecommunications employees face to face (or keyboard to keyboard) to establish respect and creditability (for LoD). Phrack was a big supporter of the Phoenix Project and published something on it immediately, including the Enhanced 911 Service document.

True to his name, The Mentor was an adult–one with a real-world job as a simulation game developer for a company called Steve Jackson Games (SJG). As part of his job, The Mentor had a bulletin board on his system called Illuminati, which was run by SJG and provided hints and an information exchange for players of these unusual and exotic computerized games. Urvile, from the Atlanta LoD cell, was a committed simula-tion game player; he and his gaming friends made use of a framework produced by SJG called the Generic Universal Role Playing System. GURPS helped create virtual fantasy worlds. SJG also published books on how to use this system, including one called *Cyberpunk*.

During this time a teenager from New York City was mak-ing a name for himself in the underground by demonstrating his dominance over the New York telephone system. When his exploits reached the attention of major members of the LoD like Erik Bloodaxe, he was quickly voted into their ranks. Thus began the career of Phiber Optik and the New York cell of LoD. As it turned out, the more genteel nature of the LoD was quickly ruffled by the street punk attitude presented by Phiber Optik and his close NYC-based affiliates like Acid Phreak.

In 1989, Phiber Optik and Erik Bloodaxe had an angry spat that resulted in Phiber Optik being excommunicated from LoD. Not to be dissuaded, Phiber Optik and his New York friends started their own group, The Masters of Deception. At first, relations between the LoD and the MoD were cordial. Eventually, though, things erupted in a nasty internecine warfare. The MoD would outlive its parent and Phiber Optik would reach a pinnacle of notoriety in the years to come.

While the hacker underground continued to find its way, another drama was unfolding within law enforcement ranks with the formation of the Chicago Computer Fraud and Abuse Task Force, one of the first cyber-anticrime enforcement groups created. They based their activity on one of the initial cyber-crime laws, the Computer Fraud and Abuse Act passed by Congress in 1986. This act, which has since been amended several times, essentially made it a crime to (1) access government computer systems without authorization and obtain information pertaining to several defense and foreign relations areas with the intent to use against the U.S. and (2) access computers of financial institutions and record financial data. (More on this in Chapter 3). The Chicago-based task force had, by 1988, decided that the Legion of Doom was dangerous and the major force behind much of the illegal hacking and phreaking activity they were tracking.

The Secret Service raids began in July 1989. Fry Guy was first. His sorties into Western Union's system and use of stolen credit cards were prosecutable violations of the Computer Fraud and Abuse Act. However, Fry Guy, although guilty, was not the intended target. Simultaneous raids were launched in

Atlanta on LoD members Leftist, Urvile and Prophet. In each case, agents entered the houses where these people lived and absconded with their computers and related equipment. PCs, floppy disks, notebooks, printers, printouts, manuals, loose documents–it was all considered evidence of hacking activity. From Prophet's house they also took a digitized copy of the E911 document. Between the time that this document was stolen and the time of Prophet's detainment, the phone company had placed the value of it at almost $80,000. Also raided were the New York City homes of Phiber Optik and Acid Phreak, which yielded similar results. But little came of those raids, other than Fry Guy, the only one arrested for breaking the law, receiving probation and community service.

Then on Jan. 15, 1990, the national Martin Luther King, Jr. Day holiday, long distance phone service went down all over the United States. This seemed to be proof of what Fry Guy had said about a LoD boast to crash the phone system during a holiday. In fact, the system crashed because of a design flaw, not outside interference. But this action further motivated an already sensitized Secret Service and Chicago Computer Fraud and Abuse Task Force to take action against the most likely perpetrator of this event–the Legion of Doom and its oracle, Phrack. Knight Lightning, the current editor, was raided three days later. As was normal for most members of the digital underground at that time, he cooperated fully, believing himself to be innocent. The federal investigators discovered the Phoenix Project BBS, which they believed incriminated both Phrack and LoD.

That bulletin board was run by Eric Bloodaxe and The Mentor. Not only did they publish Phrack, but the board had a copy of the E911 document. This incriminating instruction manual became an albatross to Phrack and the LoD. When The Mentor was raided on March 1, along with Eric Bloodaxe, his copy of the SJG Illuminati board was found to include the rule book for GURPS within *Cyberpunk*. The title immediately drew suspicion and investigators, being not well versed in gaming, surmised it was a how-to book on computer hacking. So, after relieving The Mentor of all of his computers and computer equipment (as well as Bloodaxe's) the Secret Service descended upon Steve Jackson Games.

This raid was substantively different from the others. SJG was a legitimate small business, not a residence. It had no overt ties to LoD, except for an employee, The Mentor. It had no history of computer hacking; there was no E911 document to link it to anyone from the underground. To avoid any undue destruction, The Mentor even opened the SJG doors for the Secret Service. Agents, in turn, took all of the company's PCs and related equipment. These machines retained all of the company's business accounts, as well as its current and projected game development. In a truly Kafkaesque moment, no one was arrested and no charges were levied but the systems were taken and never returned. In essence, the raids put Steve Jackson Games out of business.

The company went to the Secret Service demanding its systems back, and was told that the apprehended *Cyberpunk* was a manual for computer crime. Jackson's protestations that it was science fiction did not yield the results he wanted. This raid turned a legitimate action against computer crime suspects into what many in the hacker community called a witch hunt. A firestorm of civil liberties complaints poured down upon law enforcement officials, causing significant changes in how police dealt with computer evidence–the retention and the return of computer systems to those involved in any sort of investigation.

Operation SunDevil: Getting the Message Across

Not every raid presented the same challenges as the Steve Jackson Games case. Around the same time LoD members' machines were being confiscated, other law enforcement officials were conducting well planned and smoothly executed raids on criminals operating within cyberspace. Operation

> **"No, this is real."**
>
> **The response from the Secret Service when told that a Steve Jackson Games manual was science fiction, as recounted by author Bruce Sterling in The Hacker Crackdown**

SunDevil was conducted from May 9 through May 11, 1990. This operation employed 150 Secret Service agents as well as many local law enforcement officials. It served 30 search warrants in 14 cities across the country. It targeted computer hackers alleged to have trafficked in stolen credit card numbers and unauthorized long-distance dialing codes, and to have illegally accessed and damaged computer systems. SunDevil's targets were bulletin boards.

The sting began as a DeVry University student's senior project. Dale Drew was working part time changing oil at a Sears automotive center in Phoenix when he created a bulletin board system called The Dark Side to attract hackers. Every case within Operation SunDevil was based on the evidence that Drew collected and provided to the U.S. Secret Service over a two-year span.

"We went to a summer hacker conference in St. Louis, where the goal was to gain information on the hacker culture but to also seed some of those hackers onto our bulletin board system to build notoriety," Dale, who now works in corporate security, explained. "Some of the hackers who came on board were pretty well known and pretty notorious. That allowed us to access other bulletin board systems, and that's when we came up with the idea of basically focusing away from our bulletin board sting toward collecting information from other bulletin boards to catch illegal activity going on within those other bulletin boards."

That information from some 120 bulletin board systems across 23 states was quite revealing. The goal was to catch calling card and credit card usage, which was prevalent at the time. Dale Drew was surprised at the ease of entrance and widespread use of stolen calling cards. A person need only access these boards to find the tools necessary to defraud long-distance phone companies without getting caught.

What struck Dale most about the operation was the trust that was assumed around these open social networks that grew from bulletin boards. "Anyone who expressed an interest in committing illegal activities was accepted with opened arms. They would provide them with as much information as they possibly could." There were levels to climb to gain more access to information, but one got what was needed at the start and once someone proved to have the skills sets to commit these misdeeds, he or she could rise up that social ladder.

Dale, who later would go on to work for the Arizona attorney general's computer forensics lab, said Operation SunDevil's success came from that openness and meritocracy, where suddenly the bad guys didn't know whom to trust within their ranks. Authorities within the Secret Service used that disruption in the hacker underground's social network to its advantage during the interstate arrests. Some who followed the case, which garnered media attention, were surprised that the Secret Service, and not the Federal Bureau of Investigation, was in charge. After SunDevil, the FBI took the initiative to beef up its computer crime division.

Although the hacker/phreaker community cried foul and called this operation another witch hunt, it was, in reality a solid piece of police work founded on a long and dispassionate investigation. Twenty-five targeted bulletin boards were eventually put out of business. The raids focused on search and seizures; as such, computers and related equipment, more than arrests, were sought. In fact, only four people were arrested, and all of them because of some ancillary find of illicit drugs or firearms.

While the raid eliminated only .01 percent of the boards in existence, it did accomplish several things. First, it put hackers on notice that their criminal activity was being monitored. Second, it demonstrated that cybercrime could be investigated with good general law enforcement techniques. Finally, it publicized to both the general public and the electronics community that cybercrime was no longer being "winked at" as a victimless crime. It also opened discussions on some important issues about cyberspace that needed clarification, one being whether posting illicit information like stolen phone codes or credit cards on a bulletin board was a crime in itself.

Finally, as all well-conducted raids are designed to do, it delivered a message for all who explored cyberspace: law was being established. It was clear "a new sheriff" had arrived to bring some order to this Wild, Wild West know as the Internet.

Lessons Learned

The gains by Operation SunDevil somewhat helped quell the frenzy fueled by the previous raids on the Legion of Doom and Phrack members. The SJG crackdown by the Secret Service was certainly a learning experience for everyone involved. As one of the small number of technologically savvy investigators of that era, I was particularly pleased with the SunDevil work and used the experience of the other to learn how to better conduct these types of investigations.

We were using ancient laws created before this technology could ever be imagined. Still, both of those inaugural crackdowns on computer hackers had long-term consequences. They reinforced the belief held by some law enforcement officials that cybercrime was, at its core, criminally and not just ethically wrong. Hence, it could be successfully prosecuted with standard, tested, investigative techniques. Operation SunDevil used research, informants and undercover agents to isolate and target the boards that were most likely to be either involved in or abetting criminal activity. When they struck, it was a surgical strike. While the phreaker/hacker community wailed, there was no general uproar or clamor about rights infringement. The SunDevil investigators demonstrated a gut understanding of the new, virtual medium as a potential facilitator of crime and not as a dark and scary place full of myth and horror.

Of course, horror of somewhat mythic proportions remained a very real threat.

CHAPTER TWO

Adversity as a Mother of Invention

"It's about forensics, about getting the bad guy, and about taking care of business."

CSI television actor George Eads

The less than optimal manner in which the raids on the Legion of Doom and Phrack were conducted was a learning experience for the entire law enforcement community. Even excluding the Steve Jackson Games episode, agencies collected an eclectic mix of personal property, some of which later proved to have marginal or no relevance to any criminal investigation. They then held on to this property for exceptionally long periods of time without clear reasons, as much for a lack of understanding how to process and analyze it than for any other reason.

This was a special and seminal case. With the help of the Electronic Frontier Foundation (*www.eff.org*), Steve Jackson Games filed a lawsuit against the Secret Service. The company had been hamstrung and eventually put out of business because of the raid. All of its computers were taken, even though there was little incriminating information gathered against the actual company. The courts ruled against the Secret

Service, declaring that its actions were done out of pure meanness and ordered it to pay for damages. The verdict was embarrassing, and it illustrated the depth of law enforcement's lack of understanding in how computers could be used to commit crime. However, out of this emerged a need for precise policies to seize computers and to develop forensic analysis specific to cyber issues.

Law enforcement began evolving from those initial misunderstandings about technology and suspicions based on emotional responses. Police and federal agents often acted purely on gut instinct, believing the bad guys were doing bad stuff using technology and needed to be stopped, maybe even without following normal criminal investigative processes. This, of course, was not only incorrect but counterproductive. Understanding this technology as just a new tool that criminals could use was a first and necessary intellectual step.

The eventual outcome of these raids was decidedly mixed. They put people on notice that they'd be held accountable for their criminal activity. They also increased the visibility of other hackers and galvanized the attention of existing and new groups of civil libertarians bullish on First Amendment rights. Make no mistake: The luminous label of rebel hacker among the underground's elite was starting to dim as people on both sides of the law realized the ranks of mischievous phone company pranksters now contained real criminals using computers to conduct nefarious acts. Catching and prosecuting them required an entirely new approach to evidence identification and collection and toward technology.

More than Just a Desk Job

Any discussion on computer forensics must include Mike Anderson. Mike was a special agent with the U.S. government, who could best be described as a "cop's cop." He also was a successful entrepreneur and an avid fisherman who's now somewhat retired (at least while

> "...wait a minute, secretaries do typing! What are you doing, Anderson? Get back into the field!"
>
> **Comment made by an FBI chief after observing agent Mike Anderson doing some early computer forensic work**

the steelheads are running). He will argue with me about who coined the term "computer forensics," and we should probably just let that go. Either way, Mike was one of those there at the beginning, becoming the first federal agent to testify in U.S. District Court as a law enforcement computer expert. He was also the person who successfully received federal funding to formalize the field of computer forensics for federal law enforcement agencies. It's impossible to discuss the origins of computer forensics without mentioning Mike.

Younger generations need to take it on faith that at one time computers were odd and somewhat marginalized instruments. Prior to 1982, there were personal computers from a number of manufactures not named Apple or Dell, Toshiba or Hewlett-Packard. Prominent at that time were systems from Radio Shack, the TRS ("trash") 80; the Commodore 64-128; and products from Atari, Sinclair, Eagle, Texas Instruments and others.

This mosaic of system types confounded early attempts at computer forensics simply because each operated so vastly different from the others. At that time, not only did early cybercops have to battle against institutionalized managerial ignorance, but they also had to locate the person (often only one of a select few) with expertise in the targeted system. A Commodore guy would have to locate an Atari guy if the target system was an Atari. The common denominator at work at this time was that most of the early successful cybercops were at first computer hobbyists. This put them at considerable advantage in mustering consistent and effective approaches to cracking computer-based information that could actually stymie the criminal element.

The introduction of the IBM PC and the subsequent consolidation and standardization of personal computers solved much of the multi-vendor, multi-platform problem. Now everyone was either using a PC or Apple. However, it did not address the bigger, institutional problem: management on the force had no clue. The first breakthrough in validating the importance of computer forensics in the eyes of the law enforcement bureaucracy came during a tax fraud case conducted by the Internal Revenue Service.

The IRS, for obvious reasons, was among the first adopters of computer technology and, hence, had an appreciation of its abilities long before its organizational cousins. In a court case in the early 1980s, information believed by the IRS to be important evidence was encrypted and stored on a personal computer. Mike Anderson, who was known as a computer enthusiast, was asked if he could extract the hidden data. He could, and the descrambled data provided the IRS the information it needed for a successful prosecution. This awareness that important or incriminating information was being stored on computer files, yet ignored during routine investigations, was a watershed for the fledgling field of computer forensics.

Still, other government agencies, true to their bureaucratic nature, were not quick to fully embrace the idea that the computer was being employed as a criminal tool. Therefore, they were slow to see the need to develop and deploy forensic tactics to meet this new threat. There were several important and revealing reasons:

- Law enforcement was steeped in tradition and leaders who didn't want anything to change

- Officials didn't understand the technology and were loath to admit it

- If organizations did embrace the technology, they would have to fund it and support it, which they didn't want to do with limited resources being what they were

As a result, many of the first computer forensic cases were investigated and solved by dedicated people often working on their own time. And, like me, buying their own equipment at their own expense. The agents conducting these computer investigations took a lot of heat from their management who, more often than not, failed to understand how spending many hours "banging" on a keyboard could ever apply to real investigative work.

This attitude began to turn around in 1988 when Mike was given funding to set up formal computer forensics training at the Federal Law Enforcement Training Center. Assisting the agent were several people who later became luminaries in the computer field, such as Peter Norton (Norton Utilities, Symantec) and Mike Brown (Central Point Software). Up until then, both Mike and I conducted informal computer forensics training for law enforcement groups upon their request. This training was conducted on an ad hoc basis and often began with some very fundamental (*"This is a keyboard... This is a CPU...*") instruction. In 1989, the first 30 people graduated from the training center's computer forensics program. However, these graduates would return to field offices where management still didn't grasp the relevance of PCs within a criminal investigation and therefore failed to appreciate these skilled employees. They thought that these agents were just playing computer games. Getting top management buy-in for establishing or expanding cyberforensics remains an uphill battle even today. Now, though, it's not so much because of reticence or ignorance but because technology advances too quickly to easily stay current.

It's easy to understand the misconceptions. Computers at the time were still seen as powerful machines kept in air-conditioned, sterile rooms and tended to by strange people in white coats that spoke in strange tongues. Those consumers who owned an Atari or Commodore PC used it more for playing games than any serious application.

Federal Computer Crime Geeks Unite

FCIC, as the Federal Computer Investigations Committee was better known, had a nice ring to it. It sounded large, important, cutting edge and high-profile. Well, it was cutting edge. At its peak in the early 1990s it had about 40 members, including Mike Anderson, Dan Mares, Andy Fried and me. But

> "If the FCIC went over the cliff on a bus, the U.S. Law Enforcement community would be rendered deaf, dumb and blind in the world of computer crime."
>
> **Bruce Sterling, author of The Hacker Crackdown**

the term "member" is a bit of a misnomer. The FCIC was comprised of like-minded individuals from federal, state and local law enforcement that met three to four times a year, on our own nickel.

We met at different sites to discuss the current state of affairs in computer forensics. It started at the Federal Law Enforcement Training Center in Glynco, Georgia, and then from there it traveled around the country where the hosting agencies periodically met. We'd line up speakers to discuss issues on the emerging topic of computer crime and computer forensics.

This committee was strictly ad hoc, with no funding. Taking a lesson from the cybercriminal's playbook, we met regularly to share information on cases and to better learn how to investigate the criminal activity that was going on. This loosely ordered group played a seminal role in developing forensic techniques and equipping people with the skills needed to beat the Legion of Doom and Masters of Deception at their own game—using good, solid investigative tactics. But all of these techniques had to be developed from scratch.

That's why I decided to do this book, if initially reluctantly. By seeing what little law enforcement had to work with in those early days, you'll come to better appreciate just how far we've come.

Digging into the Hardware

So the hill was high and the wagon we were dragging was full, but we somehow still made progress, with our peers and with the technology.

My expertise was in taking a systems approach, rather than

> "It is not the mountain before you that wears you down, but the grain of sand in your shoe."
> **Ancient Chinese proverb**

a specific hardware or software approach. In the early days of the PC, hardware drove the technology and software followed (a paradigm since reversed, primarily by Microsoft's efforts). Still, much of this expertise had to be learned on the fly as hardware and software changed rapidly during this period.

Several key cases provided me with important lessons in how to research criminal computer systems to provide useable evidence. Current computer sophisticates may find the following cases somewhat quaint and obvious, but remember that all progress on this initial computer forensics was made one step at a time while staring at an empty screen and feeling pressure from several directions.

It's the Spreadsheet, Stupid

One of my first attempts at computer forensics was during a routine drug investigation. In this case, we were working a small-time crystal methamphetamine (meth) dealer. The guy was buying an "8 ball" (8 ounces) of crystal meth and selling it in quarter gram papers out of a bar within my jurisdiction in Arizona. We completed all of the standard investigations, which eventually led to a search of his house. There, we found an old IBM PC that was being used for a legitimate business conducted by the suspect. The computer was running a Lotus 123 spreadsheet—a PC spreadsheet later supplanted in the market by Microsoft Excel—that was set up to manage and monitor his drug distribution. It contained detailed data like "Spent $70 for an 8-ball from Bob," "Sold a quarter gram to Kathy," "Sold a quarter gram to Mike," etc. Being somewhat careful, he had also installed a batch file that would not run the Lotus 123 application until a password was entered. This "security" method is simplistic by today's standards, but back in the early

90s the bad guys thought of it as a good way to shield sensitive information from the police.

Typically, in a case like this, we try to get a confession. Therefore, once this dealer was apprehended, my partner began interviewing him in the interrogation room. As usual, this guy insisted he didn't know what we are talking about. He had no idea, he maintained, how the dope got into his car. Someone must have put it there. On and on it went.

Then my partner informed the guy that we had his computer system and that his partner (which was me) teaches at the FBI academy. He's going to break into that system and get all the records, the suspect was informed. Confidant in his personal security system, the guy still would not admit to anything. While this was going on, I was in another room trying to obtain evidence from this system by just rebooting it and applying some other simple forensics techniques that would be considered quite rudimentary today. I eventually was able to bypass the password, run Lotus 123 and printed out his customer and supplier list. We placed the incriminating printouts before him. He confessed to everything.

The Computer Chop Shop

It's apparent by now that computer crime differs substantively from what is considered ordinary street crime. At the beginning of the PC era, a general lack of understanding of how computer technology worked often resulted in miscarriages of justice. A good example of this is what I call the Computer Chop Shop Case.

There'd been a flurry of break-ins in businesses and homes in which computer systems were stolen. These included Apple systems, IBM PCs and the newly marketed IBM clones, a genre of PCs manufactured by a bevy of U.S. and Asian companies based on the standard Intel/DOS platform supported by IBM. Some of the best known brands today were among the successful PC clones. Systems were being stolen on a regular basis and for a while, we had no leads. Our break came when a woman entered the office stating that her live-in boyfriend was beating up on her. He was arrested for domestic violence and while he was in custody, she told us that he was a burglar running a computer chop shop. In this operation, he took stolen computer systems; switched video cards, parallel cards and other components from one system to another; printed new bars codes; and, in some cases, labeled them before they were resold as computer systems. He even had a storefront.

We finally got a search warrant based on the battered girlfriend's information. When the warrant was executed, the computer system was running and there was a file open that contained a running list of the buildings he had burglarized. This list included the type of computer(s) he had stolen, the house/business it was stolen from and the date of the burglary. This was all really good evidence and significantly incriminating. However, this slam dunk instead sunk under the weight of computer evidence ignorance. I was tied up in an undercover investigation, so one of the MIS guys (what we called IT guys at the time) from the city was brought in to do the evaluation. Unfortunately, he knew nothing about gathering computer evidence, so he saved the file to a floppy disk that was in the system, overwriting the original file. At that time, on a DOS-based computer system, it was impossible to tell anything other than the date and time the file was last saved based on the machine's time stamp. When the file was saved, it updated the date and time stamp. This then became an evidentiary issue.

When I later talked to the defense attorneys, I found out that they were going to argue that law enforcement officials had written that information on a file and saved it to disk in order to contrive incriminating evidence and clear its case load. This was feasible because the date that the file was last changed was two days after this guy was already in custody. Of course the "last change" date was when the MIS guy saved the data. The attorneys' argument was going to be that the cops had made all of this information up to make the defendant look guilty. The lawyer maintained his client couldn't have done it because he could prove he was elsewhere at the time the disk was made.

This looked like a lame excuse. However, this occurred at a time where there was a lot of distrust towards police based on recent televised video accounts that painted police with a broad brush as overly aggressive. The upshot: The guy was able to plead out and never go to trial. Still, on the positive side, with all of this evidence we were able to trace back parts directly to the victims.

Hide 'n' Seek

Following that incident with the floppy copy, we contracted with a company that had developed a program to duplicate a hard drive. This "duplicate copy" would be completed bit by bit, and the date and time stamps wouldn't be changed. With this process, a copy of a suspect drive could be connected to another system for analysis. It would be like taking a sheet of paper with rubber gloves so as to not to disturb the fingerprints. This was a major advance.

However, several unforeseen issues came into play. First and foremost, the early PC clocks were inherently inaccurate. They were battery-driven, so as the battery weakened the clock would speed up or slow down. If an owner initially correctly set the PC clock, six months later it may be minutes or even hours off. That would mean that the investigator would then have to capture the BIOS signature. (For those of you unfamiliar with this technology, investigators had to self-configure the hard drive in a system because there was no auto-configure function as there is now. This would entail identifying the number of cylinders, heads and sectors per track the hard drives had). This data had to be typed in and sometimes people would be deliberately inaccurate to build in inconsistency.

Another issue with the old DOS operating systems was that the hard drives had to be initially low-level formatted, and then partitioned and formatted using command line tools. Believe me, it was slow and tedious. People eventually learned that they could also configure this technology to make some partitions invisible.

Finally, this computing era depended on the 5 ¼-inch floppy disk drives. This technology fell out of fashion before the vinyl record, but it was the dominant storage media of its day. What we discovered was that there were programs readily available on the existing bulletin board systems that would enable changing the number of cylinders or the number of sectors per track on these floppy disks. So, for example, a floppy that normally had 18 sectors per track could be changed to have 19 sectors per track, and DOS wouldn't recognize those new sectors. When compiling evidence, some of these tools would have to be used to look for pieces of disk that were invisible to DOS.

Another tool that rose in popularity was an early version of Norton Utilities, which included a disk editor tool that could be used to mark a particular cluster of the drive as bad. The operating system then "thought" that area was defective, but in reality the physical sectors were fine and could be used to hide bank numbers or dates of drug deliveries and other devious data. Another obstacle to successful investigation was the fact that an image would have to be made of the hard drive and all suspect floppies, which could be extremely time consuming. The only saving grace was that at that time few hard drives were larger than 20 megabytes. Hence, this wasn't an overly onerous process. As a comparative example, the 5 ¼-inch floppy disk prominent then could store the equivalent of one to two paperbacks, a 200- to 300-gigabyte hard drive common today stores a good-sized library.

A Sophisticated Blackmail

One of the more interesting and elaborate criminal scams to eventually succumb to computer forensics involved blackmail. I was still working in Chandler and got a call from the FBI field office based in Phoenix. The cofounder of a nationally recognized herbal supplement company was being blackmailed.

He had an 8-year-old son and owned a minor league ball club when he received a five-plus-page letter in the mail. The outside was a common type of brown envelope with two stamps and a label made by a laser printer. Inside this envelope was a second envelope. On this was printed Personal and Confidential and it was clearly done on a dot-matrix printer. Within that envelope was a letter demanding $500,000 or the owner's son would be kidnapped and tortured. The letter made very specific references to the victim's family and business, suggesting the extortionists knew him. The criminals claimed, however, to have found the family from motor vehicle and property tax records. Another thing peculiar about this particular threat: It actually read like a marketing plan for a reputable company and not your run-of-the-mill extortion letter.

Now, the targeted businessman had aspirations that his kid would become a professional baseball player, and he'd publicized those dreams. So something about the threat of dismemberment in the extortion letter hit close to home.

In a short amount of time, the FBI developed a potential suspect. In typical fashion, one of the blackmailers became convinced that he wasn't going to get his money and dropped a dime on his co-conspirators. The lead identified a programmer working for the county in Arizona. Coincidentally, this person previously had also been an executive within the victim's company. This explained the business plan composed within the blackmail letter. In addition, this guy intimately knew his former boss's business, family and everything guaranteed to push buttons and make the threat personal.

When FBI agents began following up on this lead, they were concerned this programmer had left booby-traps or other nefarious stuff on the county computer systems. Therefore, they asked me to assist them with the investigation. During our first meeting, I was shown all the key evidence: the letter; the two envelopes; and the postage stamps on the outer envelope. Unfortunately, by this time, any thoughts of obtaining fingerprints off these documents were gone. My initial observation was that the outer label was clearly printed with the same type of printer that I was using at the time, a Panasonic KXP-4420. The inside letter had been printed on a dot-matrix printer (the dots were quite visible when viewed with a magnifying glass). In addition, the tops of the stamps and the right hand side had flat edges but the bottom and the left hand side were serrated.

So they looked like they were taken from the upper right hand corner of a large sheet of stamps.

Search warrants were obtained and we went over to the suspect's house to look for more evidence. When we arrived, we found floppy disks all over the house, including behind a toilet seat. I open up a desk drawer and found a sheet of a hundred stamps with two missing from the upper right hand corner. When you held them together they were a perfect match even to an untrained eye. We also discovered that he had a Panasonic KXP-4420 laser printer and, sitting right beside it was a Panasonic dot-matrix printer.

Still, all of this was but circumstantial evidence. More was needed.

It's obviously tedious to go through a thousand floppy disks. At that time the standard operating procedure for investigating disks was to make a duplicate image of everything on each one. In that way, any deleted files and slack space, as well as every bit of data on that disk, could be analyzed while still preserving the original disk. Doing this task for a large number of floppies was time consuming, not to mention brain-numbing. Therefore, another standard operating procedure was for the investigator to look first at the computer disks that were found closest to the computer system. Those sitting on the back of the toilet were probably not relevant. By employing this method of triage, we hit pay dirt.

When I got back to the FBI office I started processing these disks, starting with the one found on top of the computer. I made an image of this first floppy and started to analyze it. There were many files on it, but none of them appeared to be related to the case. Then I started examining the slack space (the area from the end of the file to the end of the last cluster of the file). What I found was a series of deleted file entries. When a file is deleted, it is not really deleted from the disk; on the file system being used, the first character of the file name is changed to a lowercase Greek sigma (σ). In this case, there were a number of entries that started with this sigma sign: σXTORT.doc followed by σXTORT2.doc, σXBAG.doc and σXTOPLESS.doc.

The "σ" could have originally been any one of the letters of the alphabet or any number 0 to 9. Therefore, we built a little chart that replaced this sigma with the letters A,B,C,D,E and, of course, the file name EXTORT and EXTORT2 emerged. These deleted files also had a date and time, which corresponded to the date and time of the blackmail letter. However, no remnants of the original file remained and nowhere on the original documents did the words 'we are former special forces guys' appear–as it had in the letter to intimidate the recipient. This guy was actively covering his tracks.

We concluded this guy created these documents, printed and then deleted them from the floppy disk and then copied other files to that disk. This conclusion was plausible because of a curious trait in how the DOS disk structure worked. The first file that he copied onto this disk had some extra space at the end of it. Therefore, DOS grabbed what was in memory, in this situation the erased directory entry, and saved that to the floppy disk. These remnants incriminated him.

As expected, when this guy was put in custody, he was initially not willing to admit anything. The agents, in a beautifully orchestrated Dragnet-like scene, open up their briefcases, rustled some papers and said, 'Hey, we've had our computer expert look at your computer systems. Tell us about extort.doc, extort2.doc, xbag.doc, xtopless.doc." Upon hearing this, the guy confessed to everything.

By the way, all that the agent had in that briefcase were blank pieces of paper. We had the names of the files, but not any content to associate with it.

As it turned out, the extort document (extort.doc) included instructions to pick up another document (expressed in true cloak-and-dagger fashion: "Go three quarters of a mile past the end of county road sign, go two hundred feet out in the desert and you'll see a four-arm cactus, at the base will be a rock painted red, lift up the rock and it will tell you what to do." Of course the note found there said, "Go three hundred feet to the left and there's a bucket with another letter in there.") Such was the sophistication of these blackmailers, straight from prime-time television. The document labeled extort2.doc provided more instructions that eventually led to the information on xbag.doc, which discussed the actual bag drop. The process planned within these documents was for the businessman to take all of this cash, put it in garbage bags, go to one of the local beach areas, take the money, and put it in the dumpster and leave. The bad guys would then sweep in and get the money.

This explained the first three files we found: extort.doc, extort2.doc and xbag.doc. But xtopless.doc still was a mystery. When asked about this uniquely named file, the blackmailer said that they had devised a diversionary plan to insure success. They had employed a stripper to go to the target beach at the same time that the money was being dropped off. When the ball club owner had dropped off the money, the stripper was to pull her top off to distract any FBI or police who might be watching. The blackmailer would then swoop in and pick up the money undetected. This part of the plan was eventually discarded because the stripper kept asking too many questions. Besides, even if the stripper had taken part, the extortionists would have had a big surprise. Half the investigation team was made up of women who likely wouldn't have been as distracted.

Operation Longarm

An important early application of computer forensics was used in Operation Longarm. Operation Longarm was a world-wide effort against cyber-based child pornography led by U.S. Customs. This occurred in 1993 as an investigation of a European bulletin board system on the Internet, based in Bamse, Denmark. Authorities suspected this board was being used to import printed child pornography materials to the United States. In this operation, special agents went undercover and entered chat rooms, searched bulletin boards for specific words like Lolita and then requested these distributors to supply them with pornographic material. During the investigation of the Danish bulletin board, agents discovered two more bulletin board systems supplying U.S. customers with child pornography. Once the distributors had been identified, 18 computer hard drives were copied. They contained the names of more than 16,000 individuals who had been using the bulletin boards, including several hundred individuals in the United States. In November of that year, search warrants were issued for these identified users, and 49 arrests were made.

My specific role in this effort was to conduct an analysis of suspects' computer equipment. At that time a common way to hide evidence was to alter the file extension of a criminal file. In essence, instead of allowing the application to name the file, such as a word processing document being named document.doc, they would change the extension of the file name to another application such as document.jpg. In this case concerning child pornography, if it was a .gif file renamed as .doc; the word processing software wouldn't open it. We had all these search tools available at the time to identify file types and search for specific extensions. However, using this tool alone, we were probably missing stuff. This turned out to be critical because the kiddie porn files were being transmitted under false extensions. Recipients had been previously instructed how to extract the pictures.

I did some research on about 40 different file headers and found some useful things. For example, in a .gif file viewed at the hex level, the first five characters were gif, gif87 or some other combination starting with gif. Consequently, I called my friend Dan Mares, who was then writing free software for law enforcement, and asked him to develop a tool that checked the header information against the file extension to identify a mismatch and then flag it as a suspicious file. This allowed us to isolate suspect files that had their extensions changed.

The specific system that I worked on contained some deleted files, some active files and some files that had been partially overwritten. One of the characteristics of a GIF file is that key components of the file are written at the beginning of the file. If data further down the file is corrupted (or over-written), a portion of the file might still be able to be displayed—up to the area of corruption. Utilizing these two processes, we were able to find and uncover incriminating data.

In addition to this, I was also involved in debunking a defense attorney's ploy. He had hired a computer graphic artist as an expert witness. At that time graphics applications were very high-end, with available packages costing between $10,000 and $12,000. It was not standard PC fare, as Photoshop is today. It also required some advanced skill to manipulate. So, in essence it had this aura of magic about it that was not well understood by the general public. The graphic artist was able to demonstrate for the jury how quickly he could edit a picture of a woman in a bathing suit. He could change a yellow bikini from a thong to a full-size suit, alter the length of her limbs and even morph this woman into a little girl all by using some graphic editing. The intimation of this defense was that somebody had taken a picture of an adult and by applying these techniques made them look like pictures of children.

My job with the attorney general's office was to identify and exploit the holes in that defense. First and foremost, I was able to demonstrate that when someone attempts to elongate an arm with a graphics package, at the pixel level, there are observable differences in normal color matches. Viewing pictures at this detail clearly demonstrates that they have been edited. Fortunately, the jury was savvy enough to understand the technology (something that today most 12-years-olds know intuitively), reject this defense and deliver a guilty verdict.

Oh, by the way, you may be asking, what does this have to do with cybercrime? Remember, at this time, what we know of today's Internet was then a very different, very difficult-to-use network of universities and research labs with about 50,000 nodes (compared to how many the University of Michigan has by itself today). The crime was discovered in the bulletin boards and the hardware. And that is where we were. Learning how to use these devices and trying to stay even with, maybe even a little ahead of, the bad guys.

Things were about to change, though.

CHAPTER THREE

Worming a Way Into History

"Hell, I probably have more in common with the people I target than they'd like to believe."

Quote from an early cybercop printed in Phrack

Hackers are considered to be the boogeymen of the information super highway. They assault, they steal, they disrupt, they destroy. They are nameless, featureless terrors trafficking within the most important communications medium since the telephone. They operate in groups or alone, and they often have a political, economic or just a plain anarchistic agenda. Too often this plan has a frightening strategic objective. Critical infrastructure computing systems and military battle networks are now potential trophies. These hackers are no longer just a menace to society; they are the enemy.

It didn't start that way.

What happened to a colleague of mine and pioneering cybercop, Bill Baker of Louisville, Kentucky, illustrates those simpler times.

Bill was talked into conducting an interview with a Phrack magazine "reporter" who went by the hacker handle The Grimace. The Grimace was posing as a freelance reporter for the "Law Enforcement Journal." The investigator gladly answered questions, believing they'd be reprinted in a publication for fellow officers. Instead, Phrack published excerpts of the interview, without the subject's permission. But within those words, framed by the hacker-author, was a considerable amount of reverence for Baker. This was made all the more interesting since the interview took place after both the Operation SunDevil and the Steve Jackson Games raids, so tensions were high. At one point in the article, Grimace stated that he thought Bill was probably a hacker himself before he embraced "the dark side of the Force."

High praise, indeed.

Bill Baker was a committed and successful investigator of phone phreakers and early computer hackers. But the conflict, even at this point of high tension, was not to the death. Baker and the underground were opponents, but not enemies.

Much of this lack of enmity had to do with the targets: monopolistic phone companies. The "property" being stolen was phone service and computer access, not bank accounts and military master plans. The perpetrators tended to be highly curious and irreverent; not criminal-minded and malevolent.

In essence, the person police were after tended to be a smart, bored American adolescent male with no girlfriend and lots of time on his hands.

There were, of course, bad guys. But as stated in an earlier chapter, breaking what hackers thought of as "real laws" was considered bad form. In addition, we early cybercops shared a similar passion for computers and all the other trappings of the new technology. So these first conflicts were more like intellectual jousts. The Legion of Doom and Masters of Deception were flying around the computers of the phone company "looking for stuff," with members proving their mettle by taking trophies. All the while we in law enforcement made sure certain lines were not being crossed. It was certainly annoying; it was often embarrassing; but it wasn't dangerous. It felt more like chasing kids soaping windows than armed gangs starting mayhem. The "chase" helped hone all of our abilities.

However, much more sinister activities were afoot and, as is often the case, the good guys were often a day late and a penny short. The previous chapter discussed some of the reasons why law enforcement was behind the times in adopting strong, comprehensive and proactive cybercrime capabilities. This hesitancy occurred simultaneously with the Internet's first important growth spurt and government's first encounters with shadowy hackers with more than trophies on their minds.

FBI Profile of Typical Computer Hacker in 1999

- A nerd

- A teen whiz kid

- An underachiever with stunted social skills

- Male (90 percent of the time)

- U.S. resident (70 percent of the time)

- Online an average 57 hours each week

- Believed he'd never be caught

The Department of Defense
& The Cuckoo's Egg

The aforementioned hesitancy in law enforcement at this time was only part of a dangerous mixture of behavioral disinterest in protecting cyberspace that existed in the late

> "Give me a lucky general, not a good one. Everything is to chance."
> **Napoleon Bonaparte**

1980s. Not only were potential countermeasures non-existent or in their infancy, private companies and government agencies beginning to be linked together by this "Internet" thing were mostly oblivious to their potential exposure. There were holes in the primitive security used to control access that a hacker with some knowledge and patience easily could exploit, and to great results.

This intersection of ignorance occurred with a vengeance when German hackers on the payroll of the East German Stasi, the country's fearsome secret police, gained entry into U.S. Department of Defense and other critical computers. They were thwarted by one person, working on his own while investigating a small discrepancy in usage charges. This case was named The Cuckoo's Egg by the astronomer and computer system administrator, Cliff Stoll, the hero in this case who noticed a tracking error while working at the Lawrence Berkeley Laboratory in northern California. He realized German hackers had gained "root" access to the lab's computers and used that escalated systems privilege to attack U.S. military computer systems. Stoll convinced supervisors at the Labs to allow him to set a trap that ultimately ensnared the culprit. This was in the days of ARPANET and MILNET, but the case, which later became a popular book and PBS documentary, was a seminal illustration of the early Internet's vulnerability and the general atmosphere of disinterest law enforcement displayed toward its protection.

Before discussing The Cuckoo's Egg in greater detail, this disinterest among authorities needs to be better explained. At that time, law enforcement was not structured to handle problems that crossed jurisdictions as easily and rapidly as cybercrime did using the Internet. It was never clear just who should lead in this investigation, so no one agency ever felt obliged to take the reins. Neither the Central Intelligence Agency, which should have pounced on the espionage angle, nor the FBI, which should have been interested in the nationwide scope of this crime, could find compelling reasons to jump in. Even the U.S. Air Force, whose computers were being hacked, failed to step up. Besides the inhibiting force of bureaucracy, battered by years of jurisdictional squabbles, the arcane rules of peer-to-peer computer communications left most investigators' eyes clouded over. It was not just difficult for Stoll to find someone who cared; he found it difficult to find someone who even understood and appreciated the case's ramifications to national security.

A group of hackers operating out of Hanover, Germany, broke into the nascent U.S. network of interconnected research labs and universities for entertainment and profit. The Hanover Hacker Group was being compensated for their "discoveries" by the Stasi, with the KGB-tainted money ultimately used to support members' significant cocaine habits.

This group had discovered a built-in opening within UNIX-based systems. They were able to obtain super user status and use that to find access information and passwords into other systems connected to it. By breaking into the computers at Berkeley Labs, they found a yellow brick road that led into communications with other university and research laboratories and, ultimately, to computers with the U.S. Air Force and Department of Defense. These guys had an advanced understanding of UNIX and the patience to use specific programs that would sift through databases to build password matches. All of this was possible because the real systems administrators charged with operating and protecting these systems had grown lackadaisical, and the users of these systems were oblivious to potential danger. Default settings were not changed and passwords, when set, were obvious. Also, employees who left or were reassigned often remained active in the system, opening up a large opportunity for hijacking identities. All of the oversights made these systems easy for these hackers to exploit.

But one systems administrator at the Berkeley Labs didn't ignore a 75-cent accounting discrepancy in the system. Stoll decided to track down the billing error for time a department within the campus had spent on mainframe computer system usage. Through tracing back the error, Stoll discovered somebody was hacking into the university system and using it as a launching point into the DoD systems, where the hackers believed they were going to be able to gain access to military secrets. Not only were the systems of the Air Force hacked, but also those of major contractors working on specific defense systems. The hackers were not actually stealing time on that mainframe but using it to sneak into other connected networks. This kicked out an error message because there was no accounting code to identify this type of usage.

All of this was uncovered by an amateur that had some computer expertise to aid him in his real career, as an astronomer. Through his own persistence and usually on his own time, Stoll was able to set traps and ultimately discover much about who these hackers were and what they planned. As was common in many of these early computer crime cases, investigations were conducted by an individual with minimal tools, often created on the fly and with little support from agencies that should have been much more concerned. In fact, often these investigations were done against the wishes of direct supervisors.

Law enforcement agencies in the United States and Europe eventually shut down the Hanover Hacker Group, but only after a year of persistent monitoring and badgering.

This case's importance rested not so much with law enforcement's disengagement–remember, it began with a 75-cent error, hardly enough to make a federal case–but to show how vulnerable that early Internet was, and how willingly an emerging breed of hacker could be used to exploit it by sovereignties and secret police. The value of the stolen documents and information passed on to the KGB in those last few months of the Cold War was difficult to assess. It might have been far worse if the Soviet Union had not fallen so quickly after its occurrence.

The Cuckoo's Egg demonstrated the need to better safeguard data moving through a seemingly porous network. But a bigger threat was looming, one with a wider path of destruction. Whereas The Hanover Hacker Club's exploits were like a gentle wind capable of passing into private places through cracks in windows and doors to do damage over time, this new danger was more like a tornado, capable of blowing apart an entire town—in minutes.

The Morris Worm

I have stated how different the Internet was in the late 1980s. It was a mere shadow of what the World Wide Web is today. It was still a closed system used by universities and the military for research purposes. Experimenters on this Internet had developed replicating, invasive programs, in essence primitive worms, to improve services or for other research. Then came the Morris Worm, which still reigns as champion of mal-

> "There are even those who suggest thanking Morris for his actions, as they provided a serious wake-up call to system administrators around the country. Of course, other people have pointed out that there might have been other ways of delivering the same message."
>
> **Charles Schmidt and Tom Darby, authors of The Morris Internet Worm**

ware for impacting the largest percentage of systems connected to the Internet. Within 90 minutes of its launch, 6,000 of the 60,000 machines then connected to the Internet were rendered unusable by this worm.

Knocking out 10 percent of the Internet was not front-page news then. While it was a major concern to the universities and military establishments directly impacted, it was only a footnote to the general public. Major broadcast news organizations devoted less than 30 seconds to it. If a worm of equal disruption hit the Internet today, it would take out so many services to be deemed a national, even international, disaster with far-reaching consequences for all aspects of modern life.

The irony of it all: Morris claims he didn't mean to do it.

From everything I've heard or read, the story began on Nov. 2, 1988, when a 23-year-old Cornell University graduate student named Robert Morris, Jr., wrote an experimental, self-replicating, self-propagating program and injected it into the Internet. This "worm" was part of a research project and was not designed to cause damage. Instead, it was created to invisibly spread itself to as many computers as possible without giving the slightest indication of its existence. If it had worked as expected, it would have been a tiny process continually running on computers across the Internet. Unfortunately, the code contained a bug that allowed the worm to infect a single machine multiple times, and at a rate much faster than planned.

Within hours, the worm, which contained a mere 99 lines of code, had overloaded thousands of Unix-based VAX and Sun Microsystems machines. This program, which didn't take up much processor time individually, began to strain systems as an endless stream of these processes infected the same machines. An infected machine would rapidly slow as it replicated more copies of the worm and was continually re-infected by those copies. It accomplished this by taking advantage of security lapses on systems running early versions of UNIX and SunOS, both popular at the time. These lapses allowed the worm to connect to machines across a network, bypass any login authentication, copy itself and then invade more machines. Administrators were forced to disconnect their computers from the network to keep the worm from spreading.

To his credit, when Morris realized what was happening, he and a friend developed a solution to kill the worm and prevent re-infection, which they sent anonymously over the network. However, because of the devastation the worm already had made, the network route was clogged. The message of a fix did not get through until it was too late. By then computers nationwide were reeling from the sudden slowdown, then shutdown, cascading throughout universities, military sites and medical research facilities.

The estimated cost of dealing with the worm at each installation ranged from $200 to more than $53,000, not adjusted to today's inflated dollars. Robert Morris was convicted of violating the Computer Fraud and Abuse Act (Title 18), and sentenced to three years probation and 400 hours of community service, and ordered to pay a $10,050 fine and the costs of his supervision.

As devastating as the Morris Worm was, it couldn't have happened at a better time. The Internet was small and connected only to research and military facilities. But it did point to a serious problem emerging within the network of connected communities: abysmal protections. Prior to this, the Internet community did not consider computer security as a big deal. But the success of the worm served as a watershed event to propel the Internet's so-called stewards into combining efforts to fix all the holes that the worm exploited, and to find other bugs that the worm missed. This effort led to some security standards still practiced today, according to authors Charles Schmidt and Tom Darby in *The Morris Internet Worm.*

The Morris Worm made the Internet community better prepared to handle and repel another such attack and led to the creation of the Computer Emergency Response Team (CERT/CC). The fact that no worm has since had this relative degree of success is a testament to these preparations. However, Internet security remains a central issue as more of the world's critical resources becomes dependent and interconnected through Internet-facing programs.

The Cuckoo's Egg illustrated how patient and proficient hackers could exploit vulnerabilities within networked systems and gain entrance into computers storing sensitive data. The Morris Worm provided a lesson on how exploitation of vulnerabilities

Security Changes as a result of Morris Worm

- **Limiting access to certain files on an as-needed basis.** The worm exploited the fact that the file containing the encrypted passwords of all the users was publicly readable in most systems. This meant the worm could compare a dictionary of possible passwords against the encrypted passwords in this file without triggering security warnings, which would occur if a large number of incorrect login attempts were detected. In addition, the file was usually in the same place on the systems.

- **Varying operating systems running on a network.** This is because it is highly unlikely that an infection on one machine will be able to run on a large number of different machines. Therefore, those networks with the greatest diversity have a lesser chance of being completely incapacitated by such an attack.

- **Sharing research** on something such as the worm (as MIT and Berkeley did in their attempts to decompile the program) is immensely helpful. Such a network of computer geeks and gurus ended up being on the vanguard of countering the worm.

- **Being wary of reflexive reactions to computer problems.** When system administrators discovered that the worm was using the email program Sendmail to penetrate their systems, many responded by shutting down their mail server. This proved to be a cure worse than the disease. The worm had a number of other attack methods; therefore, it wasn't really hampered by the loss of the mail utility. Meanwhile, email describing how to defeat the worm and fix the bugs was delayed because of the mail server shutdowns.

- **Logging information is vital in discovering the source of infections.** Many sites were hampered by the fact that they couldn't tell the source of the worm or how it was entering the system.

could be automated to infect a wide swath of systems almost instantly. Both events had implications for government systems, especially those within the Department of Defense. Keep in mind, though, the Morris Worm was a mindless marauder. It didn't care who it infected. More targeted efforts were soon underway.

The Rome Lab Case

The Rome Air Development Center (Rome Labs), located at Griffiss Air Force Base in upstate New York, is the U.S. Air Force's premier command-and-control research facility. Rome Lab researchers collaborate with universities, defense contractors and commercial research institutions on cutting-edge projects that involve artificial intelligence, radar guidance and target detection and tracking systems.

> "The following case study is a good illustration of the type of threat facing our Department of Defense information infrastructure."
>
> **U.S. Senate Permanent Subcommittee on Investigations minority staff statement, June 1996**

Numerous reports say that on March 28, 1994, systems administrators at Rome Labs discovered that a password sniffer (a tool used by hackers to gather legitimate users' login information) had been installed on a system directly linked to the Rome Labs network. This sniffer had collected so much password and log-in information that it had filled the disk and crashed the system, thereby notifying the administrators. The administrators contacted the Defense Information Systems Agency (DISA) and told them that the Rome Labs network had been hacked. The DISA Computer Emergency Response Team (CERT) contacted the Air Force Office of Special Investigations to report this intrusion. Special Investigations informed the Air Force Information Warfare Center.

The Warfare Center team discovered that two hackers had broken into seven different computers on the Rome Labs network, gaining unlimited access, downloading data files and placing sniffers on each system, which held sensitive research and development data, including battlefield simulation programs. More than 100 user accounts were captured and some email messages were viewed and copied, even deleted. Matters were made worse when authorities realized hijacked machines were used to launch on other military, government and research targets. They had broken into user accounts on these systems, planted sniffer programs and copied a large amount of data from them. This was a major hacking success and a critical breach in military security.

When the system security logs were reviewed, they revealed that Rome Labs initially was hacked into on March 23, five days before they were discovered. At this point it is obvious why these systems were ripe for attack. No one had reviewed these security logs for five days!

The Warfare Center set a trap and began tracing attacks back to their source. The majority were traced back to two commercial Internet service providers: cyberspace.com, in Seattle; and mindvox.phantom.com, in New York City. In an ironic twist, the individuals who provided mindvox.phantom.com's computer security were self-described former members of the Legion of Doom who'd gone straight. They were never implicated in this attack.

Eventually, this research provided the Air Force Information Warfare Center with the hackers' cyber personas, Datastream

Cowboy and Kuji. This was about as far as the system's research could go. The law enforcement team now had to rely on good old-fashioned investigative work, using informants and others who surfed the net in these same general areas. This is where one hacker's immaturity brought about his demise. Within a week of informants being deployed, one of them found Datastream Cowboy, boasting in an email that he was a 16-year-old living in the United Kingdom and enjoyed attacking military sites *because they were so insecure.* As any proud hacker bragging of his exploits, he provided the informant with his home address.

Scotland Yard was alerted and its investigations showed Datastream Cowboy was phreaking the telephone lines to make free international calls. His attack took a circuitous path through systems in various countries in South America and Europe to his eventual target at Rome Labs. From there, he was able to use the Internet to attack systems at NASA's Jet Propulsion Laboratory in Pasadena, Calif., and the Greenbelt, Md.-based Goddard Space Flight Center.

Here is where things got even more complicated. The Air Force's remote monitoring of the Seattle ISP indicated that Kuji had connected to the Goddard Space Flight Center and transferred data through an ISP located in Latvia. This connection was quickly broken. But Latvia! That was a former U.S.S.R. province. Not a comfortable place to be receiving classified information. In addition, Datastream Cowboy was accessing details of a joint project between NASA and the Air Force.

Potentially, the most serious point in this entire encounter occurred when Datastream Cowboy got access to a system in Korea through Rome Labs and downloaded all data stored on a Korean Atomic Research Institute system to the Rome

Labs' system. Initially, it was unclear whether this system was in North or South Korea. If it did belong to North Korea, the North Koreans would think that this information transfer was an intrusion by the U.S. Air Force and could be perceived as an aggressive act of war. Fortunately, it involved South Korea, which had a much better relationship with the United States.

That was the last straw. Scotland Yard gained a search warrant and found Datastream Cowboy, whose real name was Richard Pryce, logging off from another intrusion into Rome Labs. Kuji's identity, 21-year-old Matthew Bevan was discovered some time later. In other words, the biggest ever international computer crime investigation up to that time, one that posed a very real and significant security scare in the United States, was undertaken by two young hackers who, in their spare time, penetrated what should have been the most secure defense network in the world.

When this was all over, Bevan said that he was merely looking for any information he could find about a conspiracy or cover-up on UFOs. This was simplified by the *poor security* protecting the U.S. military and government systems suspected of holding this information.

For all the problems and disquiet caused by these two hackers, the punishments were light. Pryce pleaded guilty to 12 hacking offenses and paid a nominal fine. Bevan, whose father was a police officer, decided to battle it out. After numerous hearings in which the defense challenged the evidence, the prosecution decided a continued fight wasn't worth the funds and dropped the charges.

The most frustrating aspect of this entire episode was that Datastream Cowboy's entree into Rome Labs was through a password cracker program that could have been easily foiled if all the Air Force officers with access to these systems had followed orders and used alphanumeric passwords, ones with both letters and numerals. This was a CERT rule, ignored with dire consequences.

The Rome Labs case demonstrated the disregard that military users had for basic security measures, like a difficult to decipher password. They made it easy, almost unchallenging, for even a mediocre hacker to break into systems that held highly sensitive and top secret information. We should all be grateful the hackers were only interested in UFOs.

CHAPTER FOUR

Fighting 21ˢᵗ Century Crime with 18ᵗʰ Century Laws

"Attorneys are most comfortable when conservative. Either they want to do it the old way, or they want to see a herd doing it the new way. They sense (rightly) that if the whole world moves in a particular direction, the law will follow."

Benjamin Wright, author of The Law of Electronic Commerce

The Internet is a disruptive technology that has changed much of what we do on a daily basis. While disruptive technologies are nothing new, this one emerged quickly and impacted property by changing its very nature. Consequently, the laws defining and protecting property were quickly found to be inadequate or inapplicable. Some of these laws had remained valid since the Magna Carta of the 13th Century. Now the legal system, built to be slow, ponderous and deliberate so as not to make a hasty mistake, became overwhelmed.

Laws of property and evidence that had served law enforcement well for many decades were made obsolete literally overnight. Fighting early cybercrime was often akin to stopping

Desert Storm with Napoleon's Grand Armee. Issues of freedom of speech and illegal search and seizure had to be discussed in terms of this new media as well as standard legal issues of value and evidence. It has been a long, tedious and often frustrating battle, but an important one in balancing the preservation of the inalienable rights of citizens against the need to investigate and prosecute criminals.

'Like painting an airplane in flight'

In 1984, Steve Gold and Robert Schifreen reportedly hacked into the U.K.-based British Telecom Prestel messaging system. Using shoulder surfing, they gained admin privileges and explored the system, even accessing Prince Philip's personal email account. They were caught and tried. However, the UK's laws did not precisely identify this type of activity as illegal—there was no theft or attempt to defraud—so they both got off on a technicality. While this was obviously not a U.S. issue, the problem and challenge was similarly being waged here. In countries ruled by laws, the laws didn't apply in cyberspace.

A law enforcement investigation is not necessarily designed to discover that someone committed a crime—it's to gather the facts and let a judge or jury decide whether a crime occurred and if it had, what the offense was. This is a complex and tedious process that is monitored and limited by laws. The rapid inclusion of computer technology within crime scenes was an immediate test to existing legal statutes. Chapter Three discussed some important forensic activities in the early days. Much of this was with standalone, DOS-based PCs.

The next step in the evolution of cybercrime was the use of bulletin board systems. These systems, which could be accessed with modems, became a haven for major criminal activities such as stolen credit card information, pirated software and the distribution of child pornography. The original child pornography images that we were finding at that time were poor, grainy copies from books that had been circulated for years and had been copied and digitized. Consequently, an important issue of evidence at that time was whether the local system or the bulletin board had the original image.

We would identify a bulletin board system that contained child porn and complete a warrant to seize that contraband. One of the things that we recognized early on was the need for warrants to be precise. In one child pornography case, an investigator wrote a search warrant to explore a house for pictures, magazines, posters and all other standard material, as well as any computer files. When the judge questioned why the computer system was included in the warrant, he was informed that this had become a popular method to obtain child pornography. Unfortunately in this case, the suspect also used the computer system for legitimate activities, including housing files protected by journalistic privilege. So now there was protected information, unrelated to the crime, commingled with suspect material on the system. At this point, only a few prosecutors and judges were technically savvy enough to appreciate the nuances and challenges of this technology. We were extremely conservative about what we did during the investigations and careful to not create bad case law for later reference.

As we started to do more and more work with bulletin board systems, we found that the bad guys would often have a separate, private area on these boards where they placed pirated files and shareware programs. It was in these areas that child porn was being distributed. Those purchasing images were given a method to dial in and download the pornography to their personal systems. Based on these initial discoveries, the U.S. Customs office and the U.S. Postal Service caught on that the bad guys were using these boards as an alternative to sending child pornography through the mail, which constituted a postal violation. Since no affordable high quality printers were available at that time, all of these images had to be stored and viewed locally on the computer systems.

We understood that in these cases we were dealing with the communication and storage of evidence on computer systems. This meant entering and seizing the computers used in this activity. Some of the more technologically aware judges understood this scenario and agreed that there was probable cause that such images were stored on the computer system; thus, they allowed the warrant. However, many judges at that time didn't. They would ask how we knew that this particular person was conducting this activity on a computer system. In these situations, unless we had an informant or some precise logs from the bulletin board, we were not allowed to seize the computer systems. So if we didn't find pictures or other hard copy at the premises, we wouldn't have a case.

Real crimes were being aided by a legal system uninformed of the new technology. As you may recall, Chapter One noted the Steve Jackson Games case, in which this same unawareness was used aggressively by law enforcement to shut down and confiscate every system remotely associated with an alleged crime. What they had in common was lack of relevant information, but fortunately that began to change.

First Amendment Rights

We need to start here. We will also probably end here. No issue is more debated than what constitutes an American citizen's right to free speech. Now, being in law enforcement, one would think me conservative on this issue, but, for the record, we law enforcement types are also protected by these same laws. We cherish them and we want to be sure that they are there for us to speak freely ourselves. However, parameters need to be established. Child pornography is definitely not free expression. But how about listing (not using) stolen credit card numbers? What about adult pornography, which is constitutionally legal but subject to local prohibitions?

Once again, the catalyst for deciding some of these issues rest with Steve Jackson Games and the Legion of Doom. The crackdowns galvanized individuals and groups worried that individual rights were being trampled. One group formed directly in response to this and with the expressed goal of protecting electronic freedom was the already mentioned Electronic Frontier Foundation (EFF), which remains a visible organization supporting civil liberties in the online world. Two of its founding

In Crime and Puzzlement, Barlow outlines the fears that drove the development of the EFF

"Consider what happened to radio in the early part of this century. Under the pretext of allocating limited bandwidth, the government established an early right of censorship over broadcast content, which still seems directly unconstitutional to me. Except that it stuck. And now, owing to a large body of case law, [it] looks to go on sticking.

New media, like any chaotic system, are highly sensitive to initial conditions. Today's heuristical answers of the moment become tomorrow's permanent institutions of both law and expectation. Thus, they bear examination with that destiny in mind."

members were Mitch Kapor, the developer of Lotus 123, and John Perry Barlow, a former songwriter for the Grateful Dead.

These two met on a bulletin board designed for subscribers of the magazine and philosophy of the *Whole Earth Catalog* called the Whole Earth 'Lectronic Link (WELL). These publications were certainly liberal, even leftist with a flavor of and nostalgia for the hippies of the 1960s.

Some of my colleagues and I met with members of the EFF on several occasions. I believe they were surprised that law enforcement actually produced people with knowledge of this new technology who were willing to discuss these fundamental issues. Although we certainly did not see eye to eye across the board, there were some important areas of agreement—one being the need to establish clear parameters on which citizens agree and the legal system can enforce. EFF and WELL worked hard to ensure the preservation of our civil rights and they provide a useful watchdog function. I will not dwell on this issue since it rarely impacts everyday investigations, but it has been a consideration almost from the beginning. Bruce Sterling did a good job in explaining the role of law enforcement and the EFF in his book *The Hacker Crackdown: Law and Disorder on the Electronic Frontier.*

Old Concepts Require New Definitions

A basic truism is that it is difficult to make determinations on issues and events that you really don't know much about. Hence, many things we did in these early days were literally done on the fly. There was often no precedent for what we were encountering, nor an analogy that could be adopted as we struggled with these issues on a real time basis.

Several core legal concepts that were clearly defined and supported by law in the physical world had to be reconsidered for cyberspace. One was that of value. How much value do you put on two gigabytes worth of data? That data itself doesn't have any real value; its associated intellectual property does. The phone company put a value of more than $75,000 on its E911 document that it also published electronically and offered for free download. How can something be offered free and still be worth that much? The problem was that the company wished to restrict downloads to its technical staff. When hackers got in and made the download widely available, the phone company decided this was theft, grand felony theft at that. This spark ignited the initial hacker crackdowns.

A second concept had to do with trespass and theft. The analogy often used in defense of a hacker intrusion was that if a system is left open for someone to come in and look around or copy things, it is the system owner's problem. That was a major legal debate for a long time. Another analogy illustrating this dilemma is "If you go into town and leave the front door of your house unlocked but unopened and someone walks in and looks around, doesn't touch anything…is that against the law or not? Now, if I break into your house and steal nothing it is trespass; if I go in and steal something it constitutes a burglary. However, these laws did not apply in cyberspace. There were no provisions against this activity because there were no applicable laws. The hacker wasn't physically in any of the systems that they "explored."

A similar, surreal context surrounded theft. The legal and historic definition of theft is not that you take an item, but that you deprive someone else, the original owner, of the use of that item. When a hacker enters a system and copies a file, they do not deprive the original owner of its use. They merely gain this use for themselves. Did theft occur? The implications here were obviously enormous.

Criminal investigations are based on evidence. Cyberspace also presented issues with the value of evidence. What constituted "original" and hence the best evidence? Best evidence, from a legal standpoint, is an original copy. The assumption is that every copy made from the original can be tampered with. Of course, a digital file can be copied an infinite amount of times and still be an original copy. This is a concept taken for granted today, but years ago it provided a unique and confusing situation.

Another important undefined concept was jurisdiction. Where was the law actually broken? An example of this was adult pornography, protected under the First Amendment, but often left up to the individual communities' ethics and culture for local prohibition or limitation. The early bulletin board systems allowed individuals living in conservative areas to dial into a computer system and download pornography. Where did the violation occur? Was it in that high-moral town where it might be a violation of local law? The laws were inadequate in establishing a basis to identify where this activity was taking place, and therefore whether it violated law.

An even more problematic situation concerned international jurisdiction. This was illustrated by a case with the Canadian health care system. The agency had outsourced IT support to a U.S.-based company. When some potentially fraudulent activity occurred with these systems, the Canadian Department of Justice called the U.S. Department of Justice and asked for assistance in obtaining a search warrant to investigate the U.S.-based company. This raised the issue as to whether this crime occurred in Canada or in the U.S. Evidentiary rules differed between the two countries so establishing jurisdiction was critical.

These important issues hampered law enforcement and provided confusing and limited precedents that early cybercriminals were able to hide behind. Not only did the absence of good laws frustrate these early activities, but also the lack of good process and adequate resources.

Police Activity—Search and Seizure

Our job as police officers is to conduct an investigation; within it the facts must be allowed to go where they go, without slant or bias. It was therefore necessary to make sure we were learning and transferring investigative skills from our traditional cases to high technology. Central to investigating all criminals are search and seizure mandates. I mentioned in Chapter One the difficulties in getting the search warrants needed for a clean investigation and prosecution.

How do you execute a search warrant on a computer? The same way you do a general search warrant. If you are investigating drugs or child pornography, you go into a residence, provide the search warrant and gain entry. What you need to prove is that both the material you have taken and the suspects themselves reside in the home being searched. One of the standard things taken as part of the search warrant is what we call "documents indicia of residency," which can include a phone bill, heating bill, water bill or mortgage that demonstrate that a suspect lives at that address because that is where he gets his mail. With the general introduction of PCs, we began to include in the search and seizure guidelines an "indicia of occupancy including records stored in paper or electronic form," which then gave us the right to search the computer system.

In searching the computer system, we might find the suspect's resume or a spreadsheet on which he is maintaining his monthly budget. This would often raise an issue, during the suspect's defense, that this computer search was an unlawful invasion of private property. The process was not quite surgical.

The resources that we had available back then were such that the forensic processing required the seizure of all of the suspect's computers because the evidence could be stored anywhere on those systems. Once the systems were seized, all storage and disks were imaged. Then we would go through it all to determine if there was any evidence of guilt or if exculpatory evidence existed. Exculpatory evidence, also called Brady material, is information that says that the suspect is not the person being looked for.

For example, a person may be suspected of hacking into a computer system, but he and his three roommates each have an account on the same computer, which contains common files/folders for everyone's use and every user has their own personal folders accessible only by that individual's password. Potentially incriminating material, such as documents, IP addresses and hacking techniques, is found in the common folder. The computer belongs to the suspect, but because it is shared, the suspect can say with accuracy that although it is his computer and there are incriminating files, these files are accessible to everyone who uses this system.

When the accounts of the other three roommates are reviewed it is discovered that another user of the system has a folder in his private files on 'how to hack for fun and profit' as well as other incriminating files. The question becomes who is the hacker? Is it the initial suspect? His roommate? Both?

In our criminal system one of the toughest things to do is assign guilt to one person when two or more people were at the scene. There is a computer owned by the suspect with incriminating files in a common area. But his roommate's folder also has incriminating files. So the exculpatory material in the roommate's folder may mitigate the incriminating evidence that implicates the suspect. Because the roommate may be putting files in the common area, the law insists that this be revealed. If not, due process to find reasonable doubt was not completed. By searching every file we often searched private files that did not relate to the crime being investigated—was this an illegal search? If we didn't search everything, then we might fail to uncover this Brady information and hence procedurally fail in finding reasonable doubt.

These were all important issues that were defined by current law. The interpretation of these laws and the degree to which they were strictly or broadly applied to the unique conditions presented, depended on the specific individuals tasked with adjudicating the case. Without precedent and legal statute, this resulted in a legal system of men, not of laws, which ran counter to the design of the entire legal system.

What then started to happen was that we would go to the legislative affairs people and ask if they thought we had enough acceptable evidence to make a good prosecution. This is when we started to drive some legislation. We would tell the legal system what we were seeing and its impact on prosecutions and why ambiguous or non-existent legislation tied our hands. Often times the attorney general's office or the county attorney's office would submit draft legislation in concert with a case we were working. At times, these drafts would go to the state legislation simultaneously with us prosecuting a case in which this law applied.

At this time, we also formed things like the Federal Computer Investigations Committee (FCIC), where we brought federal and state prosecutors in and held seminars to talk about cases and discuss lessons learned. Attendees could then go back to their jurisdictions and ask their legislatures to enact pertinent laws. Canada was also represented at these events. A curious fallout from this committee was the growing competition between the federal legal agents, who recognized this as a federal area but didn't have the expertise to deal with it, and those of us at the state and local level that were dedicated to policing this new frontier and were gaining knowledge and expertise on a daily basis. In true bureaucratic fashion, the feds responded by ignoring us, though personally, I always had good relations with all federal law enforcement.

Police Activity–A Lack of Available Resources

During this same time, police forces were subject to many other pressures that limited their ability to apply resources to cybercrime. I would go to meetings and talk to police chiefs about the importance of training their people on high-tech crime. They would respond that they needed more basic things first. For example, one chief said that he needed to give his officers driver's training so that they didn't back their cars into yellow posts at the 7-Eleven store. Another one said that he had close to 300 officers out on workmen's compensation of which half were suspected of being fraudulent. Chiefs didn't see cybercrime as particularly important when compared to drug and gang activity. Most didn't understand that virtually every crime was ultimately going to have a technology component.

Training was also an issue. The selection process I went through to get on the police force included measuring my ability to run, pass psychological tests, drag dummies, jump through windows, push cars, etc. From this set of skills the department was able to determine what each individual's particular strength. What they were not looking for were technical skills or the propensity for those skills. The results were that few police officers in any city force were capable of conducting cybercrime investigations.

We attempted to remedy this by providing cybercrime training at the FBI academy. The problem was that, for one reason or another, about one third of the graduates never used the skills we taught them. Another confounding trend was that graduates might not have had a technology related case for a year or two after taking the class. At that time, PC technology was advancing rapidly and those changes in hardware, operating systems, email and the Internet required periodic skill upgrades. Many police forces couldn't justify such a significant expense. Hence, even those police forces that had trained individuals found that the training quickly became obsolete.

The Evolution of Cyberlaw

The enactment of laws used to combat cybercrime has been an expanding process often in response to identified criminal activity. As I have stated, we often worked a case and legislation simultaneously. The first real law that could be used in prosecuting cybercriminals was the Computer Fraud and Abuse Act passed in 1984. It was, however, quite limited in its scope since it only addressed crimes related to government computers, government data and consumer credit data. The act identified only these types of computer based-crime:

> "The clear shift to a borderless, incorporeal environment and the increased risk that information will be stolen and transported in electronic form is difficult to address by relying upon older laws written to protect physical property."
>
> **U.S. Department of Justice, the National Information Infrastructure Protection Act of 1996 legislative analysis**

- Unauthorized access to and use of certain federal data

- Unauthorized access to or use of consumer credit-related information

- Unauthorized access to a computer used for, or on behalf of, the U.S. government

Its limitations were identified and new legislation was enacted in 1986, The Computer Fraud and Abuse Act was the first comprehensive federal legislation regarding computer crimes that also covered non-government computers.

The Computer Fraud and Abuse Act of 1986

The Computer Fraud and Abuse Act has a special place in cybercrime legislation. Not only did it help establish a legal basis on which we could prosecute criminals, it also provided a cornerstone for all succeeding cybercrime legislation. What turned out to be an important legislative strategy began with this law. A decision was made not to go back and adjust every single law that could be impacted by the new technology, but to focus all of the changes and implications of cybercrime within this one piece of legislation and its amendments. This focus facilitated the implementation of laws to meet the evolving use of computers in crime, as well as crimes against computer systems and networks.

Under the CFAA...

...if became illegal to intentionally make unauthorized attempts to:

- Obtain protected information relating to national defense or foreign relations

- Obtain financial information

- Access a government-related computer

- Access a federal interest computer and obtain anything of value

- Access a federal interest computer and alter, damage or destroy information or prevent the authorized use of the computer or information, if the resulting loss is $1,000 or more or if the information relates to medical records

- Traffic in passwords with the intent to defraud

It was under this law that Robert Morris of the Morris Worm fame was prosecuted.

As computer systems and networks became more sophisticated through the end of the 1980s and early 1990s, amendments to CFAA were implemented to keep pace.

The Computer Abuse Amendment Act of 1994 expanded CFAA to address the transmission of viruses and other harmful code. It also added civil remedies (compensatory damages and injunctive and other equitable relief), expanded protection to include damage or loss by both outsiders and authorized users and criminalized certain types of reckless conduct and intentional acts.

The 1996 amendments removed the term "federal interest computer" altogether, replacing it with the term "protected computer," which widened protection to systems within the private sector. It also defined actions that resulted in denial of service as a crime.

Additional amendments were enacted in 2001 as part of the U.S. Patriot Act that addressed internationally sourced issues, but that will be addressed in a later chapter.

All activities covered by these statutes were first identified as crimes without legal definition or precedent. It was a long climb, and the summit is yet to be reached.

Electronic Communications Privacy Act

In the wake of the CFAA was another important piece of legislation: The Electronic Communications Privacy Act. The ECPA extended restrictions on government wiretaps on telephone calls to include electronic data transmissions completed by computers. This was an important amendment to a law initially designed to prevent unauthorized government access to private electronic communications.

The ECPA protects individuals' communications against:

- government surveillance conducted without a court order

- third parties with no legitimate access to the messages

- carriers of the messages, such as Internet service providers

It does not provide privacy protection to employees from their employers on equipment owned by these employers.

This act cleared up several issues. Prior to its enactment, the laws differed for different types of communications. The ECPA, stated that intercepting email in transit—even when temporarily stored—was equivalent to a wiretap.

In 1994, the Department of Justice issued guidelines for searching and seizing computers based on the recommendations of a task force in which many of us participated. While occurring some time after the seminal cases that caused so much angst across cyberspace, this initiative provided a voluntary set of guidelines including sample language and documents to help deal with computer evidence. After the initial excesses and then the legal hesitancy in seizing computers, these guidelines offered a refreshing simplicity on how to proceed.

1994 DOJ Guidelines for the searching and seizing of computers

These Guidelines illustrate some of the ways in which searching a computer is different from searching a desk, a file cabinet or an automobile. For example, when prosecutors must interpret Rule 41 (which requires that the government obtain a search warrant in the district where the property to be searched is "located"), applying it to searches of physical items is usually uncomplicated. But when they must try to "locate" electronic data, the discussion can quickly become more metaphysical than physical.

Even so, it is important to remember throughout the process that as dazzling and confounding as these new-age searches and seizures may be, they are in many essential ways just like all other searches. The cause must be just as probable, the description of items, just as particular. The standard investigative techniques that work in other cases (like finding witnesses and informants) are just as valuable in computer cases.

The evidence that seals a case may not be on the hardware or software, but in an old-fashioned form: phone bills, notes in the margins of manuals or letters in a drawer. It is important to remember that computer cases are just like all others in one respect at least: under all the "facts and circumstances," there is no substitute for reasonable judgment.

Comforting to an old cop who kind of sensed this was the case from the beginning.

After this introduction are eight sections and six appendices that fully delineate when, why and how computers can be seized. Unfortunately, this clarification occurred almost exactly at the time when cybercrime migrated from the hardware to the network.

These three statutes were instrumental in establishing the rules of the game for cyberspace. Some freedoms were taken from hackers who envisioned cyberspace as an open range free to roam. Clear lines were created and penalties attached. But also some restrictions, based on an application of citizens' rights, ensured that these laws were to be implemented with the restraint present in all US laws. The ignorance that had frustrated both technologically astute law enforcement and the users and denizens of cyberspace was finally fading.

Just in time, too. For on the horizon was the specter of real trouble. The Information Superhighway, like the Roman roads in 455 A.D., were luring vandals straight into our most critical and vulnerable systems.

CHAPTER FIVE

From Fame to Fortune

"'Cause that's where the money is."

Willie Sutton on why he robbed banks

Up to this point, most attacks were isolated incidents that affected a handful of companies here and there. However, the year 2000 was a watershed moment when all that would change—enter the automated, widespread attacks of worms and viruses, distributed denial-of-service attacks and also the new motive of financial gain.

The Internet changed the very nature of how business was conducted, and few things were as important as ecommerce technology. The lure of easy money not only motivated businesses to buy into the new sales tool, but also caught the eye of criminal hackers who quickly realized that there was real money now riding on the Web, and it was not very well protected.

Early Phishing and the Russian Invasion

Phishing is the web equivalent of the social engineering techniques employed by early phone phreakers to acquire confidential phone numbers and other information. Of course, the web hackers brought it to new heights by casting nets limited only by the size of their stolen email lists. Similar to phreaking, phishing began as a method hackers used to avoid paying for online service. In the mid-90s, Internet access was generally dialup and users were charged on a usage basis, such as $6.00/hour plus $.06/minute depending on the provider. Criminally minded hackers decided it was more cost-effective to hijack someone else's account and steal her services.

The hijack process was simple and direct. Phishing scams continue to this day, though the motives have now changed to obtaining credit card information, and I will bet that everyone who has been on the Internet for any length of time has received lots of emails of this type. The phisher sent out an email saying that there was a problem with your account and to please respond with your user ID and password to confirm your identity, or something similar. Unsuspecting respondents would send their user IDs and passwords, which would be used to dial into the system and access online resources.

Surprisingly at that time, Internet service providers were storing user IDs and passwords unprotected. Now they appear only as asterisks, but this initial careless approach to managing critical customer information later opened the door for astute hackers to steal credit card numbers.

Social engineering skills (as implemented in phishing) were one of several criminal activities finding new and more lucrative life on the Internet. Another was a program that would generate valid credit card numbers. At first downloadable from a bulletin board, and later more readily obtained on a web site, this program initially targeted American Express. AmEx was touched for an unrevealed, but significant, amount of money. This scam spurred it to improve its security, first with the hologram on the front side and later with the CVV number on the back. MasterCard and Visa later followed suit. Programs to produce valid credit card numbers for all major credit cards are still readily available and easily downloadable.

The Internet also enabled a group of Russian hackers to wire-transfer $10 million from Citibank's computer system. Vladimir Levin, a mathematician working for AO Saturn, a computer firm based in St. Petersburg, Russia, was said to have used his office computer to first hack into the bank's cash management system and then transfer money to other systems in Finland, Israel and California.

Interpol eventually caught Levin and his gang, and the authorities recovered most of the $10 million. Levin was finally extradited to the United States, tried and sentenced to prison and to pay back some $240,000 to Citibank.

Up to now, this was the most spectacular of the hacker exploits. However, Eastern Europe-based hacking for profit has been a continuing concern. There remain several conditions coalescing within this region to make it a hotbed for hackers. First is the skill level. There are many highly trained, top-flight programmers, analysts and computer engineers in Eastern Europe. Second is a stagnant economy. Since the fall of communism, jobs, even for highly skilled people, have remained scarce and wages low. Third is an ingrained, almost culturally based hacker's mentality. Many computer specialists grew up in the Soviet Union, where they were encouraged to hack systems in Western countries. Also, copies of useful software were often unavailable or prohibitively priced, so they learned how to steal them from the Internet. And hacking has only recently been made a crime. Eastern European high-tech criminals have the means, the motive and the experience to be exceptionally dangerous

cybercriminals. They have been behind many of the most audacious cybercrimes ever conducted.

As cyberpolice, we saw a lot of this early crime to which much
of the public was oblivious. In these early days of ecommerce,
private companies were discovering the vast economic advantages of doing business on the Web. Because they had a vested
economic interest in growing web-based commercial activities,
they had no desire to damper growth by allowing news of the
attacks to get out. Moreover, customers weren't impacted since
the financial institutions assumed all of the associated losses.
The size of the losses the institutions were willing to absorb
is a testament to the margins they were obtaining in this new
channel. Of course, the fact that the banks covered these losses
encouraged other hacking exploits. It wasn't until these attacks,
coupled with and popularized by auction fraud, were picked up
by the major news services that it became an issue within the
general public.

White Hats, Black Hats, Gray Hats

The hard lessons in security
learned from the Cuckoo's
Egg, Rome Labs and the
Morris Worm were lost in this
tidal wave of new companies

> "Improving the security of
> your site by breaking into it."
> **The rational behind the
> development of SATAN**

and individuals connecting to the Internet and slapping up web
sites. Even the most basic security processes were often ignored
by many companies in this mad dash. The vulnerability of this
rapidly growing network was appreciated by a new breed of
computer scientist that often straddled the legal fence. Some of
these people were reformed cybercriminals, others were entre-
preneurs who envisioned profits in building programs that

enhanced security. Still others may have played on both sides of the fence. All were hackers.

The names provided to the groups within this genre were straight out of the Hollywood Western. They were the White Hats (good), the Black Hats (bad) and the Gray Hats (we're not really sure). I think this is why Clint Eastwood always wore that funky brown hat in all of his spaghetti westerns. Stories of cybercriminals turning over a new leaf and plying their trade for the industries they once hacked is both truth and urban legend. Regardless of the hats, what these people had in common was an uncanny ability to identify and exploit system weaknesses.

One of the best known of these "hats" was Dan Farmer. Farmer is a genius programmer with a passion for security. He is most famous for the development of the Security Administrative Tool for Analyzing Networks (SATAN). SATAN was designed to help systems administrators to recognize some common networking-related security problems. It would then report those problems to the administrator without actually exploiting them.

In 1995, Farmer used SATAN to scan about 2,200 web sites. Many of these sites belonged to financial institutions and government agencies. He found that about two thirds of the surveyed hosts had major security problems. Half of these he stated could be exploited easily. An even more significant find was that less than 1 percent of these "attacked" hosts actually responded to the attacker, indicating that few systems actually realized that they had been attacked. His conclusion was that about 75 percent of all the sites that he surveyed could be broken into with very little effort.

Frustrated that most companies were ignoring these indications of severe security lapses, Farmer released SATAN for free and without restrictions. This was a controversial move since this program, which was also made easy to use, could provide even unskilled hackers with the ability to scan and infiltrate computer networks. Tough love, indeed, that left many of us wondering what the bad guys would do with such a powerful tool. Two camps formed when this program was released. One felt that he was being highly unethical by not only writing this program but also making it widely available and providing hackers with their first automated tool. The other side thought SATAN to be a valid tool needed to find system vulnerabilities. That debate still rages to this day.

Another popular program within this same class was L0phtCrack, a password-auditing tool intended for use with Windows. Its purpose was to test the strength of Windows user passwords by using brute force, dictionary and other attacks. In many cases, the user ID and password could be retrieved within twenty seconds. Although it was designed to test how secure a password was and to help in recovering lost passwords, its attraction to hackers targeting Microsoft operating systems is obvious.

For this reason, we were never sure if these guys were black hat, gray hat or white hat. L0phtCrack eventually became a company called L0pht, which eventually became @stake and was ultimately acquired by Symantec. Published reports note that Symantec is no longer selling the tool and will cease to support it by the end of 2006.

These were just two of many programs that could be used as effectively for building security as for penetrating it. But what also occurred at this time was a fundamental change in the nature of the system attacks. They migrated from the end-user system to the server. Hackers began to install programs like root kits, a set of tools that conceal processes, files or system data, enabling a hacker to maintain access to a system while avoiding detection by its legitimate users. They also quickly developed the ability to add and delete accounts and to capture data and files online. Organizational security practices were slow to respond and often primitive. Too often, user names and passwords were left out on the wire unencrypted. SSL, short for the Secure Sockets Layer protocol, was only rarely implemented so any user ID and password could be compromised with the sniffers then available. The days of security by obscurity were no longer with the advent of wide availability of these new automated security tools.

The First Denial of Service Attacks

We have to start with the Internet Liberation Front (ILF). Back in 1994, the ILF, with its revolutionary title, was a self-proclaimed group of activists united against the commercialization of the Internet by big

> "The Internet was built to be an open and cooperative system. That's its strength—and its weakness."
>
> **James Gleick, author and Internet pioneer**

businesses. Its members liked the free flow of ideas and concepts that defined the early Internet and believed, falsely as it turned out, that big capitalism would co-opt this medium for its own devices. Therefore, as numerous accounts detail, they started looking for ways to interrupt the activities of what they thought to be these corrupters. They were committed to the Internet staying a free-thinking society with few rules.

This is a quixotic adventure when viewed against what the Internet has now become. ILF goals were narrow and somewhat utopian and not to be confused with the goals of the ILF of today, that has a decidedly radical, left-wing agenda. However, the group did have some skilled hackers and were able to provide serious demonstrations of their wrath. They were notorious for two high-profile attacks in particular.

The first, and most visible, was the Thanksgiving Day attack, when they reportedly broke into computers at IBM, Sprint and Pipeline, a small New York-based Internet service provider. They took over these systems at the supervisory level and installed a program that spun off an email message every few seconds, eventually clogging the systems and shutting them down. The email message was a rant against "capitalist pig" corporations, accusing them of turning the Internet into an "overflowing cesspool of greed." The ILF claimed credit and ended the message with this scary thought: "Just a friendly warning corporate America; we have already stolen your proprietary source code. We have already pillaged your million dollar research data. And if you would like to avoid financial ruin, get the fuck out of Dodge."

The second high-profile attack occurred in early 1995, when hackers claiming to be the ILF trashed the promotional page of an interactive design and marketing company employed by MGM-UA to promote its *Hackers* movie, which included a rising star named Angelina Jolie.

Published accounts say the real-life hackers defiled a photograph of the movie's two stars by drawing on them with crayons and completing other acts of vandalism, including inserting links to actual hacker sites. They also advised viewers to see

The Net, the rival film about identity theft and corporate espionage with actress Sandra Bullock playing the geeky heroine.

Caught in the Act: MafiaBoy

In 1996, CERT published the following warning:

> *Two underground magazines have recently published code to conduct denial-of-service attacks by creating TCP 'half-open' connections. This code is actively being used to attack sites connected to the Internet. There is, as yet, no complete solution for this problem, but there are steps that can be taken to lessen its impact. Although discovering the origin of the attack is difficult, it is possible to do; we have received reports of attack origins being identified.*

In 2000, a Canadian teenager with the handle "MafiaBoy" conducted distributed denial-of-service (DDoS) attacks on systems belonging to Cable News Network, eBay, Amazon.com, E*Trade, Yahoo! and others. The attack slowed CNN's news operations for nearly two hours and within a few minutes of the attack, only 1.5 percent of customers who wanted to enter Amazon's site could. He did this by employing tools similar to those that were the subject of the aforementioned CERT warning—Syn-flooding.

The Syn-flooding technique was simple and instructions for using it widely available and downloadable from numerous hacker sites and bulletin boards. It works by distributing a software script to a large number of compromised systems. When launched, each of the systems sends a "half-open" connection to the same target. The target system is programmed to wait a length of time to allow open connections to close. Since all of these "half-open" connections are programmed not to close, the target system quickly becomes overwhelmed and is unable to conduct its regular business. It is so easy to use that MafiaBoy, according to press reports, was not even considered a skilled hacker by his colleagues. However, it is also so effective that the originator is difficult to locate. *MafiaBoy was caught because he bragged.*

He pleaded guilty to more than 50 charges. As a minor, he received a sentence of eight months in detention followed by a year of probation. He was also required to donate $250 to charity.

It is estimated that his attacks caused more than $1 billion in damages.

The tools used by MafiaBoy were neither new nor overly ingenious; the companies were just unprepared. In the rush to cash in on the success of the Internet, these organizations did not attend to their security.

Much justified paranoia began to percolate around the security of this Internet that was starting to play a prominent role in many aspects of the US economy. If a 15-year-old kid with limited hacking skills can wreak such havoc, what would happen to the Web if subjected to state-sponsored attacks?

Caught in the Act: Fluffi Bunni

About this time another type of hacker appeared, the web site defacer. These people did not attack the system, but the persona of a company. By 2000, most companies had web sites for both marketing and information dissemination.

In 2001, a group of defacers, using the name Fluffi Bunni, began to access and alter the home pages of some highly visible web/technology companies.

Emphasizing its prowess, Fluffi Bunni mainly targeted firms committed to enhancing Internet security, and, in turn, attempted to demonstrate those firms' futility. Among the victims: The SANS Institute, which trains security professionals; SourceForge, a developer of open source code; Attrition.Org, a web site dedicated to enhancing web security; and Apache, an open source code developer. In these cases, the group might replace the home page with a single image, or replace original verbiage with their own sarcastic and often ludicrous dissertations. Overall, Fluffi Bunni was likely responsible for 20 high-profile defacements.

When arrested at InfoSecurity Europe 2003, the alleged head of Fluffi Bunni, Lynn Htun, was gainfully employed at Siemens. The group has kept a low profile for the past several years since it purportedly failed to carry out a massive DDoS attack with thousands of Akamai's servers the group claimed to have originally compromised in 2001.

Caught in the Act: The Melissa Virus

The Melissa virus ran amuck on the Internet in 1999. It was insidious in that it was one of the first to be spread through innocent-looking emails that

> "A colossal mistake."
> **David Smith, creator of the Melissa Virus**

appeared to be sent by friends or colleagues. Curiously, its origin was in that other, unspoken "killer application" of the Internet, pornography. Legal pornography's transfer to the Internet from bulletin boards and other, more traditional media, was rapid and seamless. Melissa, said to be named after a stripper, was unleashed within a popular pornographic newsgroup called alt.sex and targeted Windows and Mac systems.

The virus was sent in a file called LIST.DOC, which contained purloined passwords that allowed free access to fee-based X-rated web sites. When users downloaded the file and opened it with Microsoft Word, a macro was triggered that emailed the LIST.DOC file to fifty people that were listed in the user's email address book. If the infected machine did not use the Outlook email application or have access to the Internet, the virus spread locally within the user's own documents.

In this manner, Melissa operated more as a worm than as a virus. It also spread faster than anything yet experienced. Reports of Melissa were first confirmed on Friday, March 26, 1999. In three days it penetrated more than 100,000 computers. Some companies were so badly infected that they had to take their mail systems offline. One site reported receiving 32,000 copies of the Melissa attachment within 45 minutes. It hampered, and in some cases entirely shut down, email systems for companies worldwide. Microsoft, for example, put a halt to all outgoing emails throughout the company that Friday to guard against spreading the virus.

Even though the final tally of Melissa's wrath was officially totaled (and probably understated) at an impressive 100,000 hosts and more than 300 organizations infected—and $80 million in clean up costs—it was not as bad as it might have been. Unlike the damage of the Morris Worm on the infant Web, two factors helped limit its spread.

■ It was launched in the U.S. on a Friday. This allowed companies to respond and implement inoculations over the weekend, thereby minimizing downtime.

■ The international incident response community, the antivirus vendors and the media worked in concert to notify the Internet of the danger, build an effective response to infection and communicate the solution worldwide.

Melissa's author was found quickly. David Smith, 31 at the time of his arrest, eventually had his sentence reduced when he agreed to help the FBI capture other cybercriminals. His final sentence was 20 months in federal prison, three years of supervised release with 100 hours of community service and a $5,000 fine. In addition, he was not to be involved with computer networks or the Internet unless authorized by the Court.

Melissa identified a severe vulnerability within the dominant PC email program—Microsoft Outlook. It also took advantage of users' familiarity with, and blind acceptance of, Word document attachments to email messages. Hard lessons that still need to be learned today.

Those That Got Away

The creators of two of the more virulent infections, Code Red and Nimda, were never caught. The Code Red worm was released on July 13, 2001. It attacked computers running a Microsoft web server by exploiting a vulnerability in its indexing software. The worm spread by creating a set of random IP addresses. Every computer infected would have to make its way through this same list. In this manner, the worm could re-infect systems and create such a level of meaningless communications as to create an effective denial-of-service attack.

Like the MafiaBoy attacks, Code Red exploited a well known vulnerability that already had a patch developed to counter it. However, users had been lax in implementing the patch, leaving their systems vulnerable. Code Red quickly spread across the Internet, eventually infecting more than 350,000 unpatched IIS servers. It also targeted the White House web site whitehouse.gov, which had to take one of its domain name servers offline to avoid the zombie attack. Its particular ability to re-infect systems that had been cleaned, as well as its speed, made it unique and damaging. It also spawned several copycats and cost an estimated $2.6 billion in cleanup and lost productivity.

Nimda, also launched in 2001 only a week after the terrorist attacks of Sept. 11, employed multiple penetration techniques that rapidly infected 2.2 million systems within its first 24 hours. It used scanning to look for systems that were not patched and vulnerable. It employed email addresses and used an exploitation technique that would execute even when opened in a preview plane. Nimda also had several firsts for malicious software: It was the first worm to modify existing web sites so they would offer infected files for download and the first worm to use normal end-user machines to scan for vulnerable web sites. This latter capability enabled the worm to reach behind firewalls and infect a company's intranet web sites. So many systems became infected with Nimda that the scanning and email traffic that it initiated caused denial of service to the networks that connected them.

What Code Red and Nimda had in common were their initial exploitations and footholds in the Internet were made on old, identified vulnerabilities that had not been patched. Good security practices would have minimized the spread of these worms.

The Microsoft Attacks

By the late 1990s Microsoft's market dominance of desktop software was well known. This made its software the logical target of a breed of worms that exploited vulnerabilities. Because the programs were literally everywhere, a well-placed worm could be assured of a large number of victims. Therefore, many worms and viruses of this time were designed to attack Microsoft software as a very large target of opportunity.

One of the most successful of these was Blaster. Blaster differed from Nimda or Code Red in that home users, connected to the Internet, were the most impacted. This was primarily because of how it worked; it was quick to spread, but slow to penetrate and execute. Its payload caused infected systems to crash repeatedly as they connected to a network. Companies with many PCs were often able to stop the internal spread of the worm and still have enough systems operating to download the patch and virus signatures. Home systems did not have that luxury. Before it was corralled, it had infected an estimated 1.2 million systems and reportedly caused more than $3 billion in damages.

The worm was programmed to start a SYN flood at a specific time directly against a Microsoft port and create a distributed denial-of-service attack against that site. However, Microsoft escaped the brunt of the damage because the target was misnamed.

As was the case with Code Red, Blaster spawned several copy-cat worms. These also provided a nuisance, but not to the degree of the original. Jeffrey Lee Parson, an 18-year-old from Minnesota, was arrested for creating a variant of the Blaster worm. He admitted responsibility and was sentenced to an 18-month prison term. Two other writers of Blaster variants were arrested as well, but the creator of the original worm was never identified.

The last worm of note I will discuss is the Sasser worm. It wreaked a considerable amount of havoc in Europe, but was known as much, if not more, by the fact that its developer was

Sasser's European Impact

Sasser's impact was primarily in Europe, where it was reported to have:

- blocked the satellite communications of a French news agency for several hours

- forced an airline to cancel several transatlantic flights

- caused a Scandinavian insurance company and its owner-bank to halt operations completely and close 130 of its offices

- disabled the electronic mapping service of a British agency for several hours

- disabled the four layer X-ray machines at a Scandinavian university hospital

caught through a Microsoft bounty program. Microsoft, like many of us was growing tired of what appeared to be an unrelenting series of worm and virus attacks and decided to strike back. It allocated $5 million to be used to reward anyone who provided the name of a person building software that attacked their products. This was ironic on several levels. First, the hacker community wondered why Microsoft just didn't invest this money into making its products more secure. Second, because it worked—so much for solidarity within the hacker community.

The Sasser worm attacked computers running Windows XP and Windows 2000. It spread by exploiting the system through a vulnerable network port, which made it particularly potent because it could spread without the help of the user, but it was also easily stopped by a good firewall.

An 18-year-old computer science student from Lower Saxony in Germany was arrested for developing this worm. A teenager who gained the attention of classmates by creating malicious code, the worm writer supposedly publicly disavowed writing worms after seeing the destruction Sasser had caused, and told his newfound friends he was through. But it was too late. The teen was turned in by some of those schoolmates seeking the $250,000 bounty placed upon the Sasser developer's head. Once cornered, he confessed to writing Sasser as well as other worms, but insisted that he did so when he was still only 17 years old. He was found guilty of computer sabotage and illegally altering data at German companies in 2005. Because he was tried as a minor, he received a 21-month suspended sentence.

Security through Obscurity

There is one thing that all of the worms discussed above, as well as most worms being developed today, have in common: They exploit a vulnerability in an application. Knowing this often leads to a cognitive dissonance within IT professionals and systems experts that uncovers a vulnerability.

On one hand, there is the thought of keeping knowledge of the vulnerability under wraps in the hope that no one else will stumble upon it. However, this also assumes that there is only one person smart enough to have identified this problem, which is highly unlikely. And if the vulnerability is revealed suddenly, without a fix, then it will be attacked immediately.

On the other hand is the responsibility to let the people using that application know how they can potentially become victims. Once this is done, the cat is out of the bag and hackers are free to exploit the problem. This is the continuing conversation on security vulnerability disclosure.

Most companies do a good job of disclosure, but they are also inhibited by vendor contracts and commitments to secrecy. Some work closely with the affected vendor to help provide a fix. Others reveal a vulnerability only when a fix is available, unless it is disclosed by another source. Law enforcement has been striving for responsible disclosure from affected vendors and legitimate researchers to anticipate potential attacks. Another issue is the fine line between being a legitimate whistle blower and an individual with an agenda to wreak havoc. It is impossible to get into someone's mind to determine whether they are a "white hat" researcher or a "black hat" programmer writing the exploitive code to prove a concept. These issues will be debated as long as there are vulnerabilities in software.

Yet another problem arises when a patch is released. By looking at the code, or sometimes just from reading the advisory that accompanies it, an attacker can determine where the vulnerability lies and how to take advantage of it. Hence, the time between when a vulnerability has been publicly identified and when most users have applied the fix provides an excellent window of opportunity for an attacker.

The one surety is that someone, often with malicious intent, will find that unintentional hole in the integrity of an application. Once found, it is often child's play for a good hacker to develop code to exploit it.

CHAPTER SIX

An International Affair

"I think computer viruses should count as life. I think it says something about human nature that the only form of life we have created so far is purely destructive. We've created life in our own image."

Physicist Stephen Hawking

For a period of time, cybercrimes were mostly a domestic issue. Of course, the high-profile Cuckoo's Egg event demonstrated that foreign nations were a concern, but the hacker seemed to be mostly an American breed. By the mid-1990s this began to change. PC penetration began growing in many developing nations, and the Web's international expansion was almost complete. Couple this with increasing computer savvy and the hacker nation began assuming an international persona. This raised the stakes in important ways.

Show Us Some 'Love'

While I previously noted some of the more effective worms and viruses unleashed upon the Internet, one of the more renowned viruses remains I Love You. It's reach was

"Sixty to 80 percent of its Fortune 100 clients were infected by the virus."

Antivirus software provider McAfee's research estimates

unprecedented, with more than 45 million systems impacted around the world eventually causing more than $10 billion in damages. It was one of the first viruses to employ social engineering techniques to fool users into opening an infected attachment, in this case a supposed love letter. When victims saw the phrase "I love you," they carelessly downloaded the attachment, and the virus.

Aside from the clever use of social engineering, the virus attacked a previously unexploited, and therefore unprotected, part of Microsoft Windows: the VBScripts. Once the attachment was opened, the virus would rename graphic and music files, making them difficult, if not impossible, to retrieve and use. It would then instruct the victim's browser to access a web site where a Trojan horse program would be downloaded onto the victim's computer and search for passwords it would send to an email account in the Philippines.

It also commandeered the address books of its victims and used them to send out more emails. These messages appeared to come from an acquaintance, thereby lowering the recipient's suspicion and adding incentive to open the infected attachment. Just a few users at each site opening the attachment would generate a volume of emails that would cripple email systems and overwrite thousands of files.

The origin of I Love You eventually was traced to the Philippines and, ultimately, to a student of AMA Computer University, Onel de Guzman. He pleaded guilty to developing this worm, although he insisted that it was a school project released by mistake. Since there were no hacking laws in the Philippines at the time (August 2000), prosecutors dropped all charges. This allowed the developer of one of the most destructive viruses to date to walk because there was no legal statute to convict him. This was a clear demonstration of the need for harmonization of international laws that provide equal punishments for malicious hackers worldwide.

This virus began an era of email-aware worms that continue to plague the Internet. Even after six years of attacks like these, Internet users are still susceptible to simple social engineering tricks.

A New Game in Town

Cybercrime began as a quest for fame and as a method for otherwise socially restricted young adults to strut their stuff. As the Internet expanded to become a critical factor in global commerce, the modern day highwaymen appeared, motivated to rob unsuspecting travelers on the information superhighway. These robbers had a decidedly international flavor, with hackers based in Russia, Germany and South America responsible for some of the more high-profile attacks.

> "Hacktivism bridges the realm between hacking and activism. Its champions are not motivated by the thrill or challenge of exploiting/attacking computers or their networks. Nor are they interested in making money. They believe they are activists and use their skills to make political statements and launch protests against the 'enemy' government and industry."
>
> **Priya Ganapati,**
> **author of The War in**
> **Cyberspace**

In tandem with these economic attacks for monetary gain were a growing number of information attacks against both the government and larger companies. Some of these, such as those by the Hanover Hacker's Club, were fishing expeditions for military information that could be sold to the late Soviet bloc.

Others were driven by commercial concerns. Hacking into rival corporations, especially foreign rivals, while formally frowned upon, has often been winked at. To paraphrase a former official of a foreign intelligence service: We do not spy on the U.S. government; we are allies, we are friends, but why should we pay $20 million for something commercial when we can "acquire" the technology and build it ourselves for much less?

Still others have loftier goals—to strike out against real or perceived injustices or cultural differences.

Indo-Pakistan Cyberwar

Hacktivism's origins vary, with some high-tech historians placing it as far back as October 1989 when government computers worldwide connected to VMS machines were hit by malicious code launched by anti-war protesters. Others say the modern-day version of political activism through hacking was born when the longstanding conflict between India and Pakistan extended to the Internet. The first important salvos occurred during the 1999 armed conflict between the two nations that took place between May and July in the Kargil district of Kashmir. Hackers from both sides began to deface web sites of important institutions in the rival country. Although both countries exchanged hacks during this time, it was the Pakistanis, and groups sympathizing with them, that were the most persistent. Two groups emerged as the primary perpetrators of these attacks: G-Force and the Pakistani Hackers Club. G-Force was a slash-and-burn operation that hacked high-profile government and commercial sites and defaced them with profanity, insults and tasteless jokes. This group's focus was the Kashmir issue and promoted a distinctly religious agenda.

The Pakistani Hackers Club (PHC) was formed by two "hacktivists" with the pseudonyms DoctorNuker and Mr. Sweet. DoctorNuker allegedly started hacking into critical Indian government servers with a distinct focus on nuclear and atomic sites. The PHC took a much different approach than G-Force, by carefully focusing on important targets instead of making random strikes. The group hacked the web sites of India's Department of Electronics, The Ahmedabad Online Telephone Directory, India's Parliament home page and India's United Nations sites. PHC also had a freedom-for-Kashmir agenda, but its attacks were more sophisticated and less profane.

By 2001, PHC and G-Force had combined to form the Al Qaeda Alliance, with a professed goal of supporting the terrorists and wreaking havoc among western servers, as well as stealing information and providing it to what they called the right hands. The Alliance has hit several western targets of various importance, including U.S. Department of Defense sites. Their modus operandi has been to deface these sites with political and religious statements supporting terrorism-related activities.

What began as a regional issue has now become global.

China Eagle Union

The developer of the I Love You virus was not punished because there were no local laws that established the release of malicious code onto the Internet as a crime. The Pakistani Hackers Club initially had a distinct nationalistic agenda that supported Pakistan's continual

"Western hackers probably would not recognize the Chinese Eagle Union as a hacker group. It is more like a professional association with structure, regular meetings, enthusiastic membership and specific goals."

Former security company iDefense, now owned by VeriSign

conflict with India over the Kashmir. However, the government did not officially bless this drift toward the more militaristic Islamic radicals. There were no reports that the Pakistani government punished these activities, but neither were they officially sanctioned. This is where the China Eagle Union differs; it is also what makes them potentially much more dangerous.

Earlier, I posed the question of what would happen to the Web if it's subjected to state-sponsored attacks. The activities of the China Eagle Union are the closest thing yet to state-sponsored web hacking that we know of. In 2006, Reporters Without Borders described the Chinese government as an "enemy" of the Internet. It earned this harsh title by ordering its three largest Internet service providers to spy on their users and report any unpatriotic or unusual activity. There have been several cases where Chinese hackers who defaced Chinese government web sites have been sentenced to prison terms. China has a thumb on the pulse of its hackers and shows precious little leniency.

While internal hacking is tightly controlled, there is no such control over the hacking of foreign sites. Attacks from China have been quick in response to international events.

In 1999, during the Yugoslavian civil war, NATO bombs hit the Chinese Embassy in Belgrade, killing three Chinese journalists and outraging China. Even though the United States and NATO apologized, relations were strained and the incident provoked demonstrations outside Western embassies in Beijing. It also elicited a wave of malicious hacks, which, although never proved, had a singular Chinese tone and sympathy. Government sites attacked included the Department of Energy, Department of the Interior and the National Parks Service, as well as the White House web site. These attacks were of concern, but none struck at the DoD, CIA, FBI or other more hardened sites. However, as it turned out, these were only the opening salvos.

The critical catalyst that increased both the frequency and intensity of these attacks was a collision of a U.S. surveillance plane with a Chinese fighter jet. The Chinese pilot was killed, heightening diplomatic tensions. Defacements of U.S. and other web sites ensued. There were no published reports of the Chinese government taking any actions against these China-loyal hackers who defaced nearly 1,000 web sites and launched a distributed denial-of-service attack against U.S. government sites. This also marked the appearance of the China Eagle Union (CEU) as an aggressive hacker group with international targets.

By 2002, the CEU was reported as being the major hacking group in China. Several attributes separate this group from hacking clubs in other countries. First, and most curious, is that it doesn't hide its activities; the group is open and often brags about its hacking attacks on foreign targets. While they have pseudonyms, everyone, even an American group researching them, knows their names. Second, they are composed mostly of young professionals from 25 to 35 years old. These are not the teenage eggheads with a nihilistic streak often found hacking in the West. CEU is different and must be viewed as different. Interfax China referred to CEU as *"a domestic non-profit organization that has been involved in hacker wars against Japanese and American counterparts."* Has any hacker in the U.S. ever been accused of being a non-profit?

All of this leads to the belief that the CEU operates with the tacit approval of the Chinese government. No one in the Communist government can have issue with these ongoing CEU targets:

- Japanese historical interpretation of the Sino-Japanese War

- U.S. hegemony

- Taiwan's attempt to become an independent state

Further validating CEU's position as a sanctioned enterprise is its inclusion within a state-sponsored seminar on cybersecurity. Even CEU members spoke during the same seminar as the Chinese Director of Science and Technology of the Ministry of State Security.

The CEU has brought global hacking with a national agenda to a new level, taking full advantage of the Internet as a means to strike at another country's culture and economy without employing the traditional trappings of war.

Internet Liberation Front—Redux

I noted some activities of the ILF in the previous chapter, but that was a very different group with different goals than what has recently emerged. Back in 1995, the ILF was for the freedom of the Internet and worried about this emerging media being co-opted. Now it is about perpetrating a distinct agenda. Although it claims to speak for the world of the oppressed, it has the whiny self-righteous tone of the American far left. It claims its actions are founded in social justice struggles and that it doesn't deface web sites for fun, but it is here to "make change, to bring revolutionary ideas to the people and to disrupt capitalism and government through hacktivism."

Its first high-profile attack was to deface Republican web sites during the second inauguration of George W. Bush. Regardless of your position on this administration, these hacks were attacks on free speech, and this is what is most disconcerting about the ILF. Its self-professed beliefs are "that any and all action that can cause humiliation or financial disruption to unjust corporations or governments is justified, as long as it does not bring harm to human beings, and innocent bystanders are not affected. Shifting data around in the right direction cannot only bring attention to political issues, but it can also help stand in the way of injustice and oppression." Of course, how they determine who and what is unjust is not spelled out. Chances are it will be decided by a small group, ostensibly speaking for "the people" and using their own freedom of speech to restrict or inhibit that of those with whom they disagree.

International hacker groups with a national or religious agenda are certainly a dangerous threat. However, in many ways, their motives are clear, and hence, their activities can often be anticipated and protected against. A group of avowed U.S. haters, especially those who are U.S. citizens, like the ILF, pose a random threat driven more by an individual's drive to correct real or imagined injustice than by any defined agenda.

Cyber law enforcement continues to be frustrated by the truly borderless Internet. As witnessed by the I Love You virus, any smart and persistent adolescent can wreak havoc in the first world economy, no matter where he lives. Too often, these children receive praise for their exploits while punishments have been delayed or avoided due to ineffective legal statutes. International hacktivism is sometimes "overlooked" by governments when used to promote state position. Ineffective and inconsistent international laws can easily limit the truly unbridled potential of global communications. There needs to be some concord as to what is acceptable and what is illegal among countries that wish to continue to benefit from this world-shrinking technology. Only the first steps have been taken.

The International Response

International organizations have been working on issues of international cybercrime since 1996. Three groups have offered the definitions, legal harmonizing and general good sense policies that have established a framework to effectively combat cybercrime on

> "How do you apply sovereign rules in a sovereign-agnostic Internet?"
>
> **Scott Charney, then chief of the Computer Crime and Intellectual Property Section in the criminal division of the U.S. Department of Justice**

an international basis: the G8 Subgroup on High Tech Crime, the Cybercrime Convention of the Council of Europe and the OECD Culture of Security for Information Systems.

G8 Subgroup on High Technology Crime

In 1996, the United States assumed the presidency of the G8 Lyon group. This group focuses on organized and other crime matters. As its president, the U.S. assumed the right to set the group's agenda for the next year. The U.S. proposed the creation of five working groups to focus on specialized areas, one of which was cybercrime.

Scott Charney, now vice president of Trustworthy Computing for Microsoft, was a member of this cybercrime working group.

He found that group members from other countries had a distinct lack of enthusiasm for this topic because they didn't perceive cybercrime as a significant problem. At that time, this perception was valid. Computer technology and the Internet were still very much U.S.-centric. The penetration of computers and network connectivity had been far faster in the U.S. than anywhere else, and cybercrime followed fast on its heels. The United States was the victim of most cybercrime simply because it had more interesting targets to attack. The U.S. Department of Defense was more computerized than other national defense departments, and the U.S. has always had sophisticated credit, banking and telecommunication systems. Hence, the U.S. was the hackers' target of choice.

Charney and other U.S. representatives in the group walked members through the details of some cybercrime cases that the DoJ had been working on, including attackers hacking into the DoD systems or tampering with phone systems to create unlawful wiretaps or to disrupt service. Representatives from the other countries began to understand the global significance of such attacks, and the group worked together to develop useful guides on best practices and threat assessments that would greatly influence later conventions. However, its most notable achievement was an agreement by member nations to establish 24-hour-by-7-day points of contact that understand the issues and have the authority to contact an ISP and to freeze suspect data. This will allow law enforcement to acquire the legal documents needed to meet a country's jurisdictional requirements for seizing a system or intercepting wire taps. Data could be frozen quickly and be made available as evidence.

This agreement was later validated by the European Union and is now supported by many other nations. The traditional process used for international cooperation, even with countries with which we have mutual legal assistance treaties, is too slow. To secure the support of law enforcement in another country, a request must be made that is then generally funneled through the legal attaché at the FBI office in the host country. While this is often effective with traditional crimes, it is just not timely enough when dealing with the hyper-short timeframes of cybercrime.

Without these mutual treaties, the process is even slower. A government has to go to a court, which then transmits papers to a foreign court that can give it to the foreign government, etc. In one case involving the Netherlands, a box of documents arrived five years after the request. An investigator working backwards may be able to locate the source of a cyber-attack, but that data has to be caught very quickly because it readily disappears. For example, a French ISP's business model may be to keep records for seven days. If a case emerges in the U.S. from France, the France telecom company must freeze the data within the first seven days or the incriminating evidence is most likely lost. As hackers got more sophisticated in understanding how this worked, they began to take different paths to the same international destination. This would then appear to investigators as a new case and be opened as one. Assistance would be requested each time, and each time it would arrive too late.

As important and viable a process as 24-hour, 7-day point of contact is, it still often suffers from an inability to scale to meet demand. As international cybercrime increases, a tremendous challenge is placed on this system to find a computer crime investigator who has the time to handle the problem.

For example, a computer crime detective in a large city will have the normal phishing and hacking threats as well as requirements to search computer systems in support of a homicide investigation. He may then get a call from the U.K. to support a fraud case and not have resources available to field this request; there is always the issue of resources stretched too far. I would not have wanted to call the Madrid police the day, or even within six months, after the train bombings took place to ask if they could spare someone to go check on a hacker.

The Council of Europe Cybercrime Convention

In August 2006, the United States ratified the Cybercrime Convention prepared by the Council of Europe in 2001. That document embraced a lot of the work that was done at the G8 Subgroup on High Technology Crime. The U.S. was not the first country to ratify it, and there continues to be some debate on its codicils, but for all its flaws, it provides a framework on which a global response can be mobilized against global crime. One of its core achievements was to harmonize laws that pertain to cybercrime. It began by identifying nine activities that would be considered criminal offenses.

Harmonization, at first glance, appears as an obvious and straightforward objective. The I Love You virus provided an important lesson on the need to harmonize national laws for combating crimes against the Internet. The success in prosecuting the Rome Labs' DataStream Cowboy in the U.K. under U.K. law for crimes committed in the United States is a major benefit of this harmonization around cybercrime. However, at its core, it remains highly controversial, since the slowness of the international process allows each sovereign nation to make sure that it is supporting the proper cases and protecting the rights of its citizens as it cooperates in a global war on cybercrime.

A second objective was to validate and expand the around-the-clock point of contact process developed by the GB subgroup throughout Europe.

Its third objective was to establish a set of principles for investigating and prosecuting cybercrimes.

Some major issues were addressed within these principles, such as dual criminality, rules of evidence and trans-border search and seizure. The principle of dual criminality is critical in identifying what constitutes cybercrime. It is at the core of harmonizing legal statutes around this issue, but also dives deeply into a nation's perception of citizens' rights. The example of the aforementioned Datastream Cowboy case demonstrates

Nine Activites Considered Criminal Offenses Cited in the Cybercrime Convention

- Illegal access to computer systems

- Illegal interception of computer transmissions

- Interference with data transmission

- Interference with systems operations

- Misuse of system devices

- Computer-related forgeries

- Computer–related fraud

- Offenses related to child pornography

- Offenses related to copyrights

how dual criminality works. Contrarily, a foreign country in the midst of an election once petitioned the U.S. Department of Justice to provide evidence and help arrest a person who had published something on the Internet criticizing one of the candidates—an illegal act in that country. The DoJ said no, the individual was asserting free speech that is protected in the United States. Implementing a dual criminality requirement ensures that other countries can't pass laws and remotely impose them on foreign citizens. It gives countries a way to refuse a request for assistance.

A second issue addressed by the convention is rules of evidence. In order to prosecute internationally, there is a need to develop some commonality on evidentiary rules. Does just shipping a file from point A to point B provide enough evidence for these various national courts, or are images required? Are personal

Principles for Investigating and Prosecuting Cybercrime

- International cooperation should be provided to the "widest extent possible," and impediments to investigations minimized

- Cooperation is to be extended to all criminal offenses related to computer systems, and data and to the collection of evidence in electronic form

- These provisions do not supersede international agreements, such as mutual assistance and extradition treaties

- Mutual assistance is subject to domestic laws

- The requested party must execute requests in accordance with the procedures specified by the requesting party, to ensure that the domestic laws governing the admissibility of evidence are fulfilled and the evidence can be used and data privacy laws being violated when information relative to someone's Internet usage is released? The interpretation of these activities varies widely. The convention leaves it up to the individuals working the case to ensure the proper handling of evidence. This is a suboptimal process that will be difficult to implement, especially in countries with strict rules on what is, and what is not, allowable evidence.

Trans-border search and seizure is another issue. For example, an agent in the U.S. arrests someone and sees a computer screen listing a directory of child pornography. He downloads it and saves it for evidence, not realizing that the file server is in another country and he has just conducted a search in another sovereign state. This is one of the major challenges of the Internet. In the physical world, agents know they can't go to another country, kick in a door and search a room. On the Internet there are no clues suggesting an international border has been crossed, yet sovereign rules still apply. Addressing this issue, the convention first concluded that a search of a computer system and its related components can be considered together as forming one distinct system. Trans-border access to stored computer data was also declared unilaterally permissible as long as: 1) the data being accessed is publicly available; and 2) the party has accessed this data through a computer system within its own territory.

Challenges certainly remain. Issues of sovereignty are still being grappled with because countries are loath, for obvious and good reasons, to give up sovereignty and allow such searches of systems in their control. If the U.S. had taken this position, then we might have enabled Saddam Hussein to search the DoD systems simply by issuing himself a search warrant, because enforcing the no-fly zone is a crime against

Iraq. Obviously, much work needs to be done to settle that issue. There have been suggestions for creating a world court for the Internet, but we will have to wait and see.

Creating a Culture of Security for Information Systems

The international responses to cybercrime noted above are defensive in nature and focused on how the Internet can play a role in devastating attacks. The Organization for Economic Cooperation and Development took a more proactive view of the Internet as an enabler of worldwide commerce and, hence, a target for old-fashioned economic crimes. The issue it sought to address was how to create a culture within the participating nations that was not just about public safety, but also about economic viability. The international group developed nine principles to be followed by the economic entities of their respective countries to not only combat Internet-based crime, but to build an environment that is less susceptible to it. These principles read like a set of well-known best practices.

The analogy that I use for this "culture of security" is the evolution of automobile seatbelts. I remember back in the days when we didn't have seatbelts in cars. Those cars were equipped with rock solid steering wheels that could impale you during an accident, as well as those suicide knobs on the radio that could poke a hole in you if hit hard. Over the years, and after several exposés, the auto manufacturers determined that these ever bigger and faster cars were very dangerous. They responded by adding seatbelts and collapsible steering wheels.

At first, people advised vehicle occupants not to wear seatbelts because they would impede escape if the car exploded after a crash. This reduced their use. As an incentive to get people to wear them, car companies put in an annoying buzzer that mostly caused people to hook the belts behind their backs. Then, as a culture of security began to be developed with the continual discussions about the safety of seatbelts and other devices, carmakers responded with automatic seatbelts that come across and just require a click. From there they began installing air bags and side air bags, etc.

About three years ago, I was giving a graduation speech at the University at Phoenix and I asked my grandson, who was 3, if he wanted to ride with me. He said, "Oh yeah, I want to go with you," and then he asked if I had a car seat. I told him no, and he said that he couldn't ride with me because he needed to be in a car seat. The culture of security was ingrained in him, and he wouldn't think about getting into a car without a seatbelt and a car seat. When my son graduated from the same university a couple of months ago, I asked my grandson if he wanted to ride with me and he said, "Yes, but I'm going to have to ride in the back seat unless you have the button that turns off the air bag on the passenger side." It is that type of culture of security what we are looking to embed with these OECD principles.

In the long run it will be the awareness, preparedness and responsiveness that result from implementing these OECD principles that will harden all of the targets. Moving toward more cooperation and harmonization among nations will increase the likelihood that cybercriminals will be caught and will have no place to hide.

9 Principles for Combatting Internet-based Crime

AWARENESS: Participants should be aware of the need for security of information systems and networks.

RESPONSIBILITY: All participants are responsible for the security of information systems and networks.

RESPONSE: Participants should act in a timely and cooperative manner to prevent, detect and respond to security needs.

ETHICS: All participants should respect the legitimate interests of others.

DEMOCRACY: Security should be compatible with the essential values of a democratic society.

RISK ASSESSMENT: All participants should conduct periodic risk assessments of their systems and networks.

SECURITY DESIGN AND IMPLEMENTATION: All participants should incorporate security as an essential element of information systems and networks.

SECURITY MANAGEMENT: All participants should adopt a comprehensive approach to security management.

REASSESSMENT: All participants should review and reassess the security of information systems and networks and make appropriate modifications to security policies, preventive measures and procedures.

CHAPTER SEVEN

Safeguarding Our Goods

"We have not found any new crimes as a result of the Internet; criminals are just finding new ways to commit old crimes."

Kevin Delli-Colli, Deputy Assistant Director, Financial Investigations, U.S. Department of Homeland Security

As the world becomes increasingly more wired, more people with criminal intent become wired along with it. A growing number of them are technically savvy residents in developing economies with little to lose and often with governments not particularly focused on their apprehension. The global law enforcement effort continues to require diligence, perseverance and a commitment to understanding cybercrime. The next two chapters discuss protective and preventive steps taken so far. These activities logically divide between those protecting the nation's critical infrastructure, which I will talk about at length in Chapter Eight, and all other activities, which I will discuss here. With experience as a local policeman and a member of the White House staff, I have seen these efforts from both an eagle-eye policy perspective and a ground-level, case-specific perspective. One thing that I can say is that the good fight continues—every day.

The Education of the Police Force

Although Internet crimes span the globe, the interpretation and implementation of laws to deter such activities remain most often local. The investigators on the scene have a major impact on the outcome of any crime. Local police now confront technology-enabled or -abetted crime on a daily basis. At first, police simply gathered computer-related evidence, so understanding how criminals used new technology to further their aims was critical. But now, with the Internet acting as an unwilling conduit for economic crimes like theft and stolen-identity scams, technology itself is now being victimized by worms, viruses and keystroke-loggers masquerading as legitimate programs.

From a law enforcement perspective, cybercrime is entering the mainstream and is no longer a specialization. At some point, every police officer will need to be trained in cyber investigative techniques. Just as we now train every police officer to collect fingerprints at a crime scene and how to tell if somebody is intoxicated, we now need to teach each how to handle computer evidence.

This will occur within the next few years. In many ways, it is a generational issue. The current generation is comprised of digital immigrants who learned to use the computer as adults. Many of them have never achieved a degree of comfort with the technology and can be found either worshipping it as a demigod or cursing it as a root of all evil. This group will soon be replaced by the next generation, the digital natives, who have grown up using computers and integrated the Internet into their daily lives. They do not hold the digital world in awe or fear. Their training on collecting and handling computer evidence will go more smoothly and improve more quickly.

I grew up watching the old FBI television shows of the 1950s and 1960s, and from them I gained an understanding of the value of fingerprints and how to collect them. In a similar manner, the next generation of police officers and federal agents will be much more technologically adroit, understanding, for instance, that computer evidence for kiddie porn can really be saved on an iPod video player. They will also be supported by a more technology savvy judicial system of judges, prosecutors and defense attorneys.

Raising the floor-level awareness of technology at the implementation level is core to building up the capability for making a concerted and coordinated effort to combat cybercrime. It can no longer be addressed by cyber SWAT teams; it must be handled with the same broad-based competency applied to more general, physical-based crimes against people and property.

Improving local competency is a core objective in combating technology-based crime at the grassroots level. However, crimes conducted over the Internet require federal agencies that have a national and international perspective and jurisdiction.

Making a Federal Case

As Internet crime expanded, some federal agencies, like the United States Customs Services and the FBI, responded by creating special divisions or operations with a specific focus to combat it. Other groups, including the Secret Service, the Department of Justice and the United States Postal Service, have provided significant resources in support of multi-agency operations targeting cybercrime.

U.S. Customs Services

Customs has been a pioneer in fighting cybercrime since becoming involved in child pornography investigations. The agency began investigating child porn after the Child Protection Act of 1984 was passed. In 1988, an amendment outlawed the use of computers to manufacture, transmit, distribute or store child pornography. Customs led 1993's Operation Longarm, one of the first successful investigations into child pornography on the Internet.

In 1996, Customs created a Cyber Smuggling Center to further combat child pornography. During their investigations, Customs agents identified evidence of other crimes being committed on the Internet, such as money laundering, intellectual property theft and the trafficking of weapons of mass destruction. In response, the center divided into three groups: child pornography investigations; cybersmuggling-type activities; and computer forensics.

Customs' jurisdiction includes anything that crosses the border, whether inbound or outbound. Since the Internet, by definition crosses many borders, even if virtually, Customs' legal jurisdiction in this medium is limitless.

The Federal Bureau of Investigations

In 2002, the FBI created a cyber division. Its mission is to coordinate and manage FBI investigations of federal violations in which the Internet, computer systems or networks are targets of terrorist organizations and foreign intelligence operations, or used in abetting criminal activity. In addition, this division helps establish the FBI as a leader in cyber investigations through staying on top of emerging technology. It also works with various public and private organizations to maximize counterterrorism, counter-intelligence, and law enforcement cyber response capabilities.

The priorities of the cyber division are to:

- Investigate and prevent computer intrusions

- Investigate computer-based crimes such as fraud, child predators and pirating of the nation's intellectual property

- Work closely with the private sector

How far we've come can be demonstrated by today's agenda. Cybersecurity is now the third-ranking priority of the FBI, behind only terrorism and espionage. Cybercrimes as defined by the FBI include: hacking, malicious code (viruses, worms, spyware, etc.), distributed denial-of-service attacks, intellectual property violations and computer-facilitated fraud and phishing/pharming (in which criminals con people into divulging financial information online).

One of newest initiatives has been the Internet Crime Complaint Center, developed in cooperation with the National White Collar Crime Center. This provides a reporting mechanism for cybercrime victims and a central repository to track and analyze Internet-related crimes.

The cyber division also is responsible for preventing online criminals from using the Internet to steal, defraud and otherwise victimize U.S. citizens, businesses and communities. This broad mandate allows the FBI to be involved in numerous operations across almost the entire spectrum of cybercrime. These will be detailed below.

The Department of Justice also has a new division, Corporate Crime and Intellectual Property Rights, which provides federal focus on intellectual property right violations and attacks on critical infrastructure.

The Virtual World's Real-Life Consequences

Some of the original battles against cybercrime involved large-scale law enforcement crackdowns with the objective of shutting down numerous perpetrators of a similar crime while creating enough shock and awe throughout that entire criminal community to dampen its efforts for a period of time. The Steve Jackson Games and Operation SunDevil raids, both discussed earlier in the book, were two prominent examples of this. As crime took on an international flavor, law enforcement operations required cooperation between both national and international agencies to be successful. Operation Longarm, in the 1990s, stopped a child pornography ring headquartered in Denmark. Major crackdowns against multi-national operations continue today. The size and breadth of these operations usually require multi-agency cooperation, both internally and internationally. They can be simply categorized as general operations against cybercrime or more specific operations against child pornography and intellectual property rights.

Child Pornography

The U.S. Customs Services has taken the lead in investigating pedophiles' use of the Internet. First was Operation Longarm, which opened with bulletin boards in 1988 and closed in 1993. It was followed up with Operation Tholian Web, based on a Swiss national's online ad for child pornography. Both investigations provided the foundation on which the Cyber Smuggling Center was established in Fairfax, Virginia. Agents from this center were responsible for conducting the London-based Operation Cheshire Cat, which was initiated in 1996 and targeted a group of child pornographers, who called themselves the Wonderland Club and traded pictures and films on the Internet. Working with British law enforcement, authorities uncovered an international web containing more than 200 pedophiles.

Within a similar time period, the FBI began conducting Operation Innocent Images. This was another large-scale investigation of child pornography and pedophile activity operating through the Internet. The objective was to identify those individuals who used bulletin boards to recruit minors for sexual relationships or distributed pornographic images of minors. Innocent Images ultimately yielded 186 convictions.

Within the morale boost that came with each operation's success lay something more sinister: The fact that child exploitation was running rampant, and stopping this brand of criminal would take continual diligence.

Intellectual Property Rights

In tandem with the emergence of ecommerce came the rise of copyright theft. With more countries involved in the day-to-day operations of U.S. corporations via partnerships and outsourcing, the opportunity to illegally copy digitized products, such as software, music, movies and electronic games, was substantially heightened. Billions of dollars in lost sales, royalties and other copyright-related fees resulted from pirated and

pilfered files illegally downloaded, often from legitimate looking peer-to-peer file sharing sites. The entertainment industry
in particular demanded stronger enforcement of digital copyright protections, which fell under controversial, wide-reaching
legislation created in 1998 known as the Digital Millennium
Copyright Act.

Operation Buccaneer was a 15-month undercover investigation
led by U.S. Customs Service and the Department of Justice to
investigate international copyright piracy, starting in December
2001 and targeting the U.S., Great Britain, Australia and the
Scandinavian countries of Sweden and Norway. It targeted the
"warez" community, an organized network of software pirates
suspected of copying billions of dollars of proprietary computer
software and offering it free over the Internet. A few years later,
three other huge crackdowns–Operation Site Down, Operation
FastLink and Operation Digital Gridlock–also honed in on
copyright infringement and software piracy. All sought to shut
down the illegal software being circulated by some individuals
within groups known as Fairlight, Kalisto, Echelon and Class,
just to name a few examples.

Collectively, these operations at the turn of the century helped
stem the tide on illegal downloading that had become quite
pervasive in the mainstream as many consumers did not initially realize they were breaking the law when grabbing free
music or movies or other software from P2P file-sharing sites.
In addition to the arrests, the recording and movie industries
conducted their own hunts for major offenders, many located
on college campuses, and began public awareness campaigns to
reduce demand for these unlawful copies.

It certainly helped that these operations, conducted by different law enforcement consortia and led by the FBI, netted

numerous arrests and have led to some two dozen convictions to date. Protecting intellectual property rights is core to conducting commerce on the Internet. Piracy of digitized information is a big business that is unofficially sanctioned in a number of countries. These high-profile operations illustrate U.S. law enforcement's commitment to crack down on those who both spread and retain unlawfully gained materials.

While copyright piracy has a large financial impact on the economy, that crime primarily impacts corporations, not consumers. Individual Internet users have their own villains and thieves to ward off while surfing the World Wide Web, which in the past decade has become rife with outlaws and predators that take advantage of the typical home user, student or employee's naiveté.

The General Assault on Cybercrime

The FBI-initiated Operation E-Con in January 2003 was the first broad, nationwide dragnet aimed at taking down any criminal that victimized Internet users. Some of the nefarious activities included in this broad-based operation were auction fraud, non-delivery of goods and services offered online, credit-card fraud, investment fraud, business fraud and identity theft. This wide net was cast by employing 43 U.S. attorneys' offices, the country's postal inspection service, the Treasury Department's Secret Service, the Bureau of Immigration and Customs Enforcement, the Federal Trade Commission and state and local law enforcement authorities. That's in addition to 32 FBI field offices located in major cities across the nation.

At the time of that particular crackdown, 48,000 Internet-related complaints had been filed with police and 263,000 with the FTC's consumer complaint hotline. Operation E-Con snared an eclectic mix of scammers, phishing expeditions and outright thieves.

There were many others, of course, some who typically used fake online orders at U.S.-based retail web sites, first shipping to legitimate addresses in the United States and then forwarding to a foreign address. Or others, who used fake email notices from financial institutions to link victims to malicious web pages that recorded private financial data used to later drain accounts. By executing more than 70 search-and-seizure warrants, 130 individuals were arrested and convicted and more than $17 million netted in seizures and recoveries, according to initial reports released by the Justice Department in 2003.

Sampling of Those Captured by Operation E-Con

- A Los Angeles man who reportedly ran an elaborate scheme to defraud computer sellers by setting up a fake company online and then steering prospective customers to a sham escrow company he created, also with a fully featured web site. The escrow web site made it appear that he had deposited the funds to be held in escrow, so the computer sellers would ship their products to him.

- A husband-and-wife team in San Diego allegedly operated a fraudulent "Russian dating" scheme directed at lonely men worldwide. Authorities said the couple took $600,000 from more than 400 victims who answered personal ads during a three-year period.

- An Illinois defendant who is said to have persuaded 50,000 people to pay a $30 to $45 registration fee to set up an at-home envelope stuffing business. The scam artist lured the victims through the Internet and direct mailings and raised $2 million before he was caught.

Operation E-Con was followed up by Operation Cyber Sweep in 2003, which utilized a similar coalition to target other crimes, such as fake escrow services on eBay and other auction sites, Internet "fencing" operations and identity theft. To continue the pressure, Operation Web Snare was initiated in June 2004 to investigate cases of denial-of-service attacks, computer hacking, the sale of counterfeit software, phishing and identity theft. These operations were intended to show cybercriminals we were on to them and not letting up. No longer could cybercrimes be conducted without fear of retribution. These were real crimes with real consequences–and a real chance of getting caught.

The Jurisdictional Labyrinth

The legal response to cybercrime in the United States has been a good news/bad news story. The good news is that many organizations are now entering the arena to combat cybercrime. The bad news is also that many organizations are entering the arena to combat cybercrime. Many agencies look to grab a piece of this investigative pie, especially where the FBI's jurisdiction is disputed. The rationale of some of the currently involved agencies is better than that of others.

The U.S. Customs Services has declared jurisdiction in child porn cases based on the fact that much of this material was being imported from international locations. For cases involving international transport, its jurisdiction is without doubt. But how about the case where child porn is developed in Portland, Oregon, and then sent to someone in Billings, Montana? That is not a clear-cut customs issue. But the Customs Service has interpreted its jurisdiction as anything that has the border as a nexus. Strictly interpreted, that would mean that all computer systems, of which a vast majority of its parts are manufactured internationally, would be within that jurisdiction. Taken to the extreme, that would encompass all cybercrime. Customs certainly doesn't actively pursue this extreme jurisdictional interpretation, but it was that type of rationale that provided them with the cash needed to set up its Cyber Smuggling Center.

The Postal Service jurisdictional claim is based on its prosecutorial efforts on illegal items being sent through the mail. This extended to encompass wire services and crimes related to companies like Western Union. It has categorized the Internet under this same "wire law."

The Secret Service is involved because of the role of access devices such as PINs and ATM machines. They have jurisdiction over them because they are part of the financial industry that falls under the Treasury Department, which includes that protective agency. Now under the post-9/11 U.S. Patriot Act, these agents also have the authority to do intelligence investigations.

It is a good thing to have many organizations paying acute attention to cybercrime. However, there is still precious little inter-agency cooperation. My worry is that these multi-agency task forces–many led by the FBI or Secret Service—that are conducting cybercrime operations like those cited above will not be in tune with, nor appreciate, the bulk of the work that is still done at the local level. I fear that some day a cybercatastrophe will occur because the existing disorganization between agencies was so acute that the evidence collected by the various jurisdictions was not shared and, therefore, the necessary electronic dots could not be connected

The table below illustrates just some of that jurisdictional overlap.

Adding complexity to these jurisdictional responsibilities is the fact that too often a cybercrime is not easily categorized and may fall across several classifications. Also, excluded from the jurisdictional responsibilities displayed in the chart below are state and local law enforcement agencies, who often engage in the street-level investigations, as well as the Internet Crime Complaint Center that often is the first to receive a complaint.

Primary Agency Jurisdiction					
CYBERCRIME	**FBI**	**SECRET SERVICE**	**CUSTOMS**	**POSTAL INSPECTION**	**DCIO**[1]
Computer Intrusion (i.e., hacking)	■	■			■
Password trafficking	■	■			■
Copyright (software, movie, sound recording) piracy	■		■		
Theft of trade secrets	■				■
Trademark counterfeiting	■		■		
Counterfeiting of currency		■			
Child Pornography or Exploitation	■		■		■
Child Exploitation and Internet Fraud matters that have a mail nexus				■	
Internet fraud and SPAM[2]	■	■			■
Internet harrassment	■				■
Internet bomb threats	■				■
Trafficking in explosive or incendiary devices or firearms over the Internet[3]	■				■

1: Defense Criminal Investigative Organizations, such as the Air Force Office of Special Investigations, Army Criminal Investigations Division, Naval Criminal Investigative Services, and other military branch's investigative units that probe cybercrime-related incidents.

2: Federal Trade Commission and Securities and Exchange Commission also have jurisdiction in specific areas.

3: Bureau of Alcohol Tobacco and Firearms also have jurisdiction.

Source: Department of Justice

The definitions of these crimes are just broad enough to make precise jurisdictional assignments a judgment call. Building an effective deterrent to these crimes is too important to be bedeviled by inter-agency squabbles. This is especially critical when the target migrates from money and other economic scams to threats on the nation's critical infrastructure.

CHAPTER EIGHT

Where We're Most Vulnerable

"Are we fully alerted to the danger now?"

Former U.S. Senator Sam Nunn, Chairman Armed Services Committee, during a June 1996 hearing that discussed a possible, devastating digital strike to the nation's critical infrastructure

Between the time the World Wide Web entered general use in 1993 and the dot-com boom began in 1997, a massive cloud of complacency surrounded users in this emerging, vibrant online community. Not only were millions of individuals and companies linking to new communications media, so were major components of the nation's critical infrastructure. I led a team of high-tech investigators as a director of the Air Force Office of Special Investigations' Computer Forensic Lab and Computer Crime and Information Warfare Division when we were assigned to attend U.S. Senator Sam Nunn's special subcommittee of the Senate Armed Services Committee on Security in Cyber Space. Begun in 1996, this subcommittee proved to be a powerful catalyst for the federal government's growing role in protecting critical infrastructure from cyberattacks.

Getting an Earful

Central to the subcommittee's convening was an alarming report prepared by the Government Accounting Office, the auditing arm of federal government. The GAO had been asked to review how vulnerable Department of Defense computer systems were to outside attack. What it found was systems already were being compromised routinely–and without notice. The GAO estimated that at that time DoD systems were attacked about 250,000 times per year, with less than 1 percent of these attacks being detected. Attackers had been successful not only in stealing and modifying information, but also in disabling entire systems and networks. And even more worrisome was the fact that less than 50 percent of those that were detected were reported to anybody.

These attacks were coming at a time when the DoD started to heavily rely on an extensive and complicated information infrastructure for most of its core activities, from identifying and tracking enemy targets to managing payroll. The Pentagon and its military operations also were increasing use of the Internet for communications, including sensitive, but not classified, data. Thus, security breaches posed a serious risk to national security and were already costing the agency hundreds of millions of dollars annually.

The specter of an "electronic Pearl Harbor" (a term I don't like, though it's used by many) started cropping up in conversations and political speeches. This vision of a potential cataclysmic attack on critical Defense systems and other networks vital to the nation's functioning was not assuaged by the findings of Nunn's subcommittee, either.

I have detailed the findings of these two committees because they illustrate the depth and breadth of this problem a mere 10 years ago. Not only were attacks successful, they were not even noticed. And when the rare breach did get some attention, efforts were made to keep it from being publicized. This was one of several important challenges identified. Another was the need to create a high level of security awareness and commit-

Findings of Nunn's Special Subcommittee of the Senate Armed Forces Committee

- The nation's information infrastructure was increasingly vulnerable to computer attack from a variety of adversaries

- The technology that allowed these adversaries to exploit networks was becoming more available and user-friendly

- The software and hardware running on these mission-critical systems and others were not designed with security in mind; thus, they were rife with flaws that provided ample opportunities for attacks

- These attackers often crossed national boundaries to conduct their misdeeds, using both private and public computer network systems and creating complex and novel legal issues

- Government and private industry were not doing enough, if even anything, to foster a culture that promoted computer security

- The government couldn't even adequately define the scope of the threat because of this head-in-the-sand approach

- Meantime, the private sector has been unwilling to report vulnerabilities for fear of losing customers and suffering severe revenue losses

- The nation is in need of a comprehensive strategy that addresses the vulnerability of our information infrastructure

ment within both the public and private sectors and encourage–if not downright demand–everyone to work in tandem for the common good and not just for competitive advantage.

The Administration Responds

Fortunately, this congressional clarion did not go unheard. The Clinton Administration took these recommendations seriously and in 1996 created the President's Commission for Critical Infrastructure Protection (PCCIP). This commission brought together informed members of law enforcement, the Pentagon, private technology developers and user groups to more fully assess the issues outlined by the Committee on Cyber Security and propose solutions to harden the protections surrounding the networks running the nation's critical infrastructure.

> "To ensure the protection of our critical networks and systems, we must work as partners, true partners, with the private sector, with the academic world, with great institutions such as this (Lawrence Livermore Laboratories), in this vitally critical effort for this nation."
>
> **Janet Reno,
> Attorney General under
> President Bill Clinton**

The PCCIP studied five economic sectors: information and communications; banking and finance; energy; distribution; and vital human services. What they found was a dangerous world becoming more unsafe every day.

Adding urgency was the fact that the American way of life, even its survival, was increasingly dependent on fully functioning computer networks that controlled electric power grids, water treatment plants, air and highway traffic control, public safety and myriad other services. These networks were created with both homegrown and off-the-shelf software and hardware containing holes serious enough to disrupt and even shutdown vital services. These same networks' complexity and interconnectivity multiplied exponentially as the Internet matured and technologies allowed for more automation and greater efficiency. Attackers were aware of this growing dependency and technological dysfunction and handily struck. No longer was the enemy some pale-skinned kid holed up in his bedroom. Now, intrusions were being launched by disgruntled employees and organized criminals abroad seeking to steal or sabotage for a variety of reasons. The threat grew, too, from terrorists, foreign intelligence operations and other technically savvy cells to engage in information warfare.

The most disturbing observation was that much of this wrongdoing was not getting the attention it warranted by the most susceptible companies providing these vital services. The attacks, whether just attempts to breach a firewall or to enter through a backdoor, weren't registering when network administrators read through event logs. Or if they did, the reports never got the needed attention from management. As such, there was no sense of urgency on a local, let alone national, level. A framework of nationwide deterrence and prevention was required.

This, of course, is not easy to do. Almost 85 percent of the nation's critical infrastructure is in private hands. Deregulation opened up once unresponsive, semi-monopolistic industries like telecommunications and power generation to market forces. While good for consumers seeking lower prices and more choice, it was bad for promoting any type of cooperation and information-sharing. Still, these sectors need to overcome some of these petty competitive skirmishes in order to develop a comprehensive method to secure the critical infrastructure that is in their care.

Recommendations made by the PCCIP were put into operation by Presidential Decision Directive 63, which President Clinton unveiled during a commencement address to the graduating class of the U.S. Naval Academy in May 1998. PDD 63 created a nationwide structure focused on protecting critical infrastructure from cyber and other attacks.

The presidential directive set off a flurry of activity. By this time, I was no longer with the Air Force Office of Special Investigations but had taken a job as software giant Microsoft's chief security officer. Given Microsoft products' rising ubiquity worldwide, and thus products' and the company's simultaneous rise as a prime target for hacking activity, I was quite busy. However, this initiative was extremely important to me, and I remained involved in seeing that the measures within those executive mandates were made real.

In 1998, immediately after the publication of this directive, led by the White House we started to conduct a series of "critical infrastructure road shows" to create momentum for private-sector support. We held one at the White House and others at large companies, such as software provider Oracle, in Silicon Valley. This was basically an awareness meeting to bring in the private sector and inform enterprises that since their IT software runs the power plants, the electric grids and other infrastructure critical to the nation's well-being, they needed to be aware that more is at stake than just fixing bugs. They needed to better understand and step up responsibilities. Given I was at Microsoft at this time, it showed many of the Microsoft executives what many of us thought had been obvious: that many of these applications run on Microsoft platforms and could be

Nationwide Structure Created to Protect Against Cyberattacks

- A national coordinator whose scope of influence includes critical infrastructure, foreign terrorism and threats of domestic mass destruction

- A National Infrastructure Protection Center located within the FBI to gather representatives from numerous agencies, the Intelligence community and the private sector to share information on threats, mitigation techniques and collaborate on improving the security climate

- Sector-specific Information Sharing and Analysis Centers to confidentially gather more accurate data on the number and severity of threats within certain industries

- A National Infrastructure Assurance Council drawn from private sector leaders and state/local officials to provide guidance on a national plan for countering cyber threats

- A Critical Infrastructure Assurance Office to provide support to the national coordinator's and to the private sector in developing a national plan and help spread education and awareness of threats

used as a portal for an attack. We needed to pay more attention to the security of these products.

You Can Drag a Horse to Water...

Information-sharing sounds like a win-win proposition. It isn't. Or at least it is not perceived that way by companies whose competitive advantage is built, at least in some part, on their ability to manage or control it.

> "We need somebody in the industry to champion this, because we are getting nowhere."
>
> **Richard Clarke, White House national coordinator for cybersecurity issues**

In 1999, Richard Clarke, the national coordinator for cyber-security issues, called a meeting with AT&T, Cisco Systems, Microsoft (represented by me), Citibank and eight other companies at the Windows on the World restaurant atop the World Trade Center in downtown Manhattan. His message was that the government had established this skeletal structure to start securing networks controlling critical infrastructure. There had been a lot of discussion, but little action. The government had been spinning its wheels and needed someone in the industry to really champion and drive the idea. At that point, I leaned over to Ken Watson, representing Cisco, and told him that I was willing to kick in some time if he was willing to match it. Knowing we were both busy, by teaming up we could pool our resources to move this project forward.

Out of that offer began the coalition between a former Marine Corps officer and a former cybercrime investigator representing two goliaths in the high-tech industry. Ken had previously been assigned with the military to the Air Force Information Warfare Center (AFIWC), now known as the Air Force Information Operations Center. We were neither pure government guys, though we had knowledge of government, nor were we pure private-sector guys, though we both had worked in private industry. We understood the challenges facing both sides and were able to bridge that credibility gap between these sectors and provide the leadership necessary to get public-private partnerships in the form of the first Information Sharing and Analysis Centers, better known as ISACs, and the Partnership for Critical Infrastructure Security. The White House was quite pleased that Microsoft and Cisco were joining forces so industry leadership could better protect critical infrastructure. Out of this relationship, and working with other industry leaders, came the Information Technology ISAC, upon which other industry-specific groups would form.

Today, in addition to IT ISAC, sector-specific ISACs now extend to the chemical, energy, emergency management, financial services, multi-state, public transit, surface transportation, telecommunications and water industries. Companies who battle each other with hammer and tong in the marketplace have found common cause in sharing information on system intrusions and potential vulnerabilities. The ISACs are now a significant structural bulwark in the fight against cybercrime.

Even though I was working at Microsoft, and the Justice Department was in the midst of legal action against the company for anti-trust violations, U.S. Attorney General Janet Reno asked me to join her department to create bi-coastal road shows promoting cybersecurity called Cybercrime Summits. Attorney General Reno very much favored building up cybercrime investigative capabilities. Given my background in law enforcement, cybercrime, defense, intelligence and the private sector, this was a natural fit to work with Dick Clarke and others in the administration to enhance the awareness of the need for cybersecurity. They believed I could be an honest broker. I didn't have a particular axe to grind and I had been in the field literally from the beginning.

The White House and National Security Strategy

President George W. Bush appointed me vice chairman of the President's Critical Infrastructure Protection Board (PCIPB) in December 2001. Richard Clarke was named the chairman. This board built upon the structure put in place by the PCCIP and PDD 63 and provided the beginning of a national strategy for protecting critical infrastructure. PCIPB was responsible for recommending policies and coordinating programs for protecting the information systems of critical infrastructure, including emergency preparedness communications. Its broad mandate included outreach to the private sector, liaison with other government agencies, information sharing, incident coordination, law enforcement coordination and international information protection. It included the heads of, or representatives of, all federal-based legal, military and economic agencies. Remember, this was just after the nation witnessed planes striking the World Trade Center and Pentagon on Sept. 11, so security concerns were at a fever pitch.

PCIPB Created 10 Standing Subcommittees Focused On:

- Private Sector and State and Local Government Outreach
- Executive Branch Information Systems Security
- National Security Systems
- Incident Response Coordination
- Research and Development
- National Security and Emergency Preparedness Communications
- Physical Security
- Infrastructure Interdependencies
- International Affairs
- Financial and Banking Information Infrastructure

To balance the workload, Dick Clarke and I spilt oversight of the subcommittees with five apiece. One of the first things that we did after I arrived was to reach out to the private sector. What assurances were there that the information on where they were vulnerable would be held safe? How would the proprietary information they shared be shielded from the press filing Freedom of Information Act requests? But the whole concept, from the start, was the need to develop this strategy in concert with the private sector, since these industries (with all the questions) own the majority of the resources.

What questions, we wanted to know, did industry leaders need answered if they were to help us create a national strategy to secure cyberspace. We received more than 300 questions. Many were concerned about purposely or unintentionally divulging corporate secrets. While trying to gain better cooperation from private industry, we also had to contend with other government entities that didn't always grasp our goals. After 9/11, many working in government believed most of our investigative energy should be put toward anti-terrorism, and that this cyberstuff was simply fighting off viruses and worms. They didn't understand how technology now was embedded into every facet of our society. So there were people actually trying to derail this effort, if only to divert more resources elsewhere. Besides battling this lack of understanding of the issue, there were also entities, both private companies and government agencies, trying to spin their activities to garner publicity, while others wished to be excluded because they did not have a good story to tell. There were also those companies still unsure their cooperation wouldn't turn on them and provide proprietary information to competitors or lead to blaring headlines.

Needless to say, trying to accommodate all these groups, and allay all these concerns, took some doing.

We decided to release a first draft of the national strategy to the public at an event at Stanford University on Sept. 18, 2002, and then conducted a series of town hall-like meetings to both gauge reaction and gather more input via a special section of the White House web site. We then tried to synthesize all of that information into the final version of a national strategy.

The first iteration of the strategy was approximately 160 pages long, which was considered way too large. So we reduced that draft into something less prescriptive, believing it provided what people needed to take action on their own. We coordinated with everybody that had an interest in this area–every agency and influential individual we could—in the time we had.

Completing this project was probably the hardest work I'd ever done in my life. Much of the success of this effort can be attributed to David Howe and Paul Nicholas. David at the time was chief of staff with the President's Critical Infrastructure Protection Board, and these two men would be at it until 1 or 2 in the morning, especially when we got to the final stages. Both played enormous roles in getting this strategy through various bureaucratic hoops. They would argue with White House staff, who often times were in superior positions, for keeping–or not adjusting–specific elements of the plan that were strongly supported by Dick Clarke or myself. They were in a very tough position and responded admirably.

The final version of the National Strategy to Secure Cyberspace was released by the White House in February 2003 and received a lot of criticism because it was not a tactical plan. Somehow, the term "strategy" in the title escaped critics' notice.

As a strategy, it discussed high-level solutions, not specific ways to accomplish objectives. It was, for a government document, a brief 76 pages that outlined a multi-faceted approach to safeguarding the nation's most important technologies.

This strategy has become the framework upon which many private and public entities now operate. The activities of the National Infrastructure Advisory Council and the ISACs related directly to these broad objectives. At some point we are going to have to update this strategy, but for now, the high-level points and the recommendations made within it are goals and objectives that people aspire to meet.

The Department of Homeland Security has assumed much of this strategic responsibility. However, there is a part of the overall initiative that's owned by the State Department in conjunction with DHS. A national security systems component is the responsibility of the Department of Defense and National Security Agency, along with DHS. And a financial systems component falls under the Department of the Treasury

The National Strategy to Secure Cyberspace Set 5 National Priorities For Development

- A National Cyberspace Security Response System

- A National Cyberspace Security Threat and Vulnerability Reduction Program

- A National Cyberspace Security Awareness and Training Program

- National Security and International Cyberspace Security Cooperation

- A More Secure Cyberspace

as the sector leader, while an IT component falls under the Commerce Department's domain. In other words, responsibility for several important areas rests with the departments that have the expertise in those core competencies. DHS is the agency who brings them all together and coordinates their activities.

Why We Can't Cry Wolf

As the percentage of citizens with a working knowledge of the Internet grows, the fear of one event taking down the entire structure or wreaking havoc on one of several critical systems seems to grow with it. A system failure causing a nuclear plant meltdown. An uncontrolled launch of a nuclear weapon. Both keep people up at night. Is it possible for one of these events to happen? Sure. Is it likely? Absolutely not. The bottom line is that we do have vulnerabilities in much of our infrastructure globally, not just in the U.S. But we have come a long way in mitigating the likelihood of a cyberevent causing real problems, and if one does occur, the simple fact that we are now paying attention will dramatically shorten the time required for mitigation.

Effective response to any disaster is based on preparation. Our system is based on a free market economy, so we are faced with another potential source for failure when company profits are not invested to the degree necessary for optimal security. On the public side, we need contingencies for when manmade or natural disasters strike, such as a hurricane or severe blizzard that causes widespread system failures.

The effectiveness of an organization is interwoven with its systems' operational efficiency. The major developers of software applications were brought to the White House and sternly lectured that their responsibility is not solely to their stockholders, but also to the people depending on the products and services driven by the applications they create. It's far past the time, they were told, to embed security into the development lifecycle. We're still trying to get that message across, I'm afraid.

We have done a lot of work, but more needs to be done before we can even begin to think about relaxing. However, we also need to maintain some perspective. I have spoken before about the Morris worm. This unintentional assault still holds the record for impacting the largest number of connected systems, about 10 percent of all machines then attached to an infant Internet. Today, worms or viruses that impact the number of systems infected by the Morris worm are almost daily events. The anti-virus software and intrusion detection appliances now routinely in place at enterprises are good enough to contain most outbreaks and quickly mitigate their damage. This may not be an ideal situation, but it keeps the system functioning at an acceptable level. I liken it to the burglary rate in a big city. In any given week, 100 burglaries may occur. As law enforcement, this may not be ideal, but it is what happens at a certain level of resource allocation. If this level begins to increase to 125 or 150 burglaries, then it's a cause for alarm—and more resources or new techniques.

The issue becomes one of threshold. When does a real problem exist?

Here are two examples. In 2002, a flurry of cyberintrusions occurred. The then-Deputy Secretary of Defense, who was a major proponent of cybersecurity, believed it important to let reporters know of this problem. Unfortunately, he had been given some overblown information that these viruses were of the most egregious, most technically savvy type and probably a sophisticated state-sponsored attack. In reality, the culprits were some teenagers from Livermore, Calif., with some computer skills and time on their hands who'd created a common virus. But once the reporters, who were unschooled in the intricacies of security technologies, got the story, they began to inflate it. They got on the national evening news and said that a new virus was released and that it was expected to take down the entire Internet by the weekend.

Wrong! Not even close.

A lot of hype ensued and then, nothing happened. Those comments were made with bad information from people who didn't know the difference between a sophisticated attack and a run-of-the-mill email exploit.

A second example involved assessing the seriousness of an attack on critical infrastructure. In November, 2002 we experienced what appeared to be attempted distributed denial-of-service attacks on the DNS servers–the machines that essentially maintained the basic underpinnings of the Internet. If this attack was successful, the Internet would start to fracture within 24 hours because it was restricting efforts to publish IP addresses and other items that had changed within the past 24 hours. By doing this, a wave of failure-to-forward errors would be generated. We held an emergency meeting and asked the DNS operators why they didn't call and notify us about this intrusion. Their answer said it all. "You want to be notified for what? We get attacked a hundred, a thousand times a day. Where is the threshold?"

Where is the threshold, indeed? For those new to cybersecurity, all worms and viruses look catastrophic. For the old hands, they appear like the run-of-the-mill attacks we were used to seeing. One skill that continues to require development as we go forward will be the ability to discern the real danger from a growing volume of cyber white noise.

The worse threats, though, are the ones that remain unidentified. Often conducted by a highly sophisticated network of hackers hired by organized crime, they quietly compromise unprotected computers and turn them into armies of what we now call bots. These botnets then do the real damage, but in small enough numbers to never register on anyone's radar. At times, these intrusions demonstrate a distinctly similar modus operandi, either on their selected targets or method of attack, so that they appear to be conducted by the same individual or group of individuals. Like the monsters in your imagination, these phantoms can take on a persona of an unrelenting danger that easily surpasses their true capabilities. We must guard against this. But we must also be willing to admit that sometimes they are real.

A Reported—but Unverified—Attack

In 2003, the news media widely reported a series of what appeared to be well-organized attacks referred to as "Titan Rain" and allegedly directed against our military and other government networks. In many ways, this is the sum of all fears–a non-random attack by a

> "Most hackers, if they actually get into a government network, get excited and make mistakes. Not these guys. They never hit a wrong key."
>
> **Shawn Carpenter,**
> **systems analyst**
> **countering the**
> **"Titan Rain" intrusions**

group of what appeared to be skilled hackers with the objective of stealing all kinds of information. This group allegedly gained access to numerous U.S. networks, including those affiliated with defense contractors, national laboratories, arsenals and space agencies. The extent of the information stolen has not been revealed, but it is reported that they took specifications for aviation mission-planning systems for helicopters and the flight-planning software used by the military, as well as thousands of armed forces documents of unknown classification.

Published reports said the origins of this attack were not known and apparently the hackers were good enough to get in and be out within a short period of time without leaving much of a trace. Much of this information comes from published interviews with a systems analyst at Sandia National Labs, Shawn Carpenter, who in true Cliff Stoll fashion began investigating these attacks on his own time. It was already understood that information collected by the hackers was being sent to a specific foreign country. However, the generally porous state of most of this particular country's systems did not mean that's where the hacking originated, nor that the information stayed there. Carpenter's analysis appeared to support the theory that the hacking activity was from multiple hackers with highly developed skills. The conclusion was that this could have been a concentrated effort, but that still needs to be determined.

The incident was eerily similar to another series of intrusions with similar government targets and select universities and research labs over a three-year period beginning in 1998. These alleged intrusions were given a case name Moonlight Maze and were eventually traced to a mainframe computer in Eastern Europe.

Are these the harbingers of the digital Pearl Harbor first discussed back in 1996? The targets of the attacks appear more an effort to collect information that can be used or sold than to actually compromise critical systems. However, the aplomb shown by these international hackers in breaking into what should be our most secure systems must give us pause. State-sponsored hacking is bad enough, but hacking for hire poses an even graver threat.

What could organizations or other groups with a suicidal commitment to our destruction, accomplish with this level of access? Diligence is required, unrelenting diligence by all entities entrusted with the nation's critical infrastructure.

CHAPTER NINE

The Highway Ahead

"I'm a great believer in luck, and I find the harder I work the more I have of it."

Thomas Jefferson

The future is often forecast by looking at or extrapolating from the past. Technology has thrown a wrench into this process as new devices and capabilities provide unpredictable opportunities for mischief. Forecasting events often focus on the wrong issues. Arthur C. Clarke's *2001: A Space Odyssey* predicted manned space missions to Jupiter and a continuing Cold War with the Soviet Union by the new millennium. It's difficult to predict what may happen, whether in the near future or the far-off one. Trends are fragile things that can easily be diverted. Therefore, my position has been that once you forecast, you are probably wrong. But let's look at my record so far.

The CERIAS Security Visionary Roundtable

In 2001, I attended a roundtable co-hosted by Accenture (then Andersen Consulting) and Purdue University's Center for Education and Research in Information Assurance and

Security (CERIAS). Also included on the panel were experts in the security industry: Rebecca G. Bace; Whitfield Diffie; Daniel Deganutti; Daniel Geer; Michael J. Jacobs; David A. McGrew; John W. Richardson; Fred Piper; Marvin Schaefer; Eugene Spafford; and Phil Venables. In addition were Accenture's John C. Clark, Anatole Gershman and Glover T. Ferguson.

After several days of discussion, the panel came up with a Top Ten list of trends impacting security. The list on the opposite page is from the Accenture report created in 2001 from that roundtable. How do you think we did?

The fascinating thing, to me, about those forecasts is our accuracy. There's little we missed. What we may have under-estimated is the use of the Internet as a means to promote an aggressive state-sponsored political agenda. This is one area where cybersecurity will need to pay more attention.

Building trusted environments using the Internet remains a difficult task and inhibits many users from conducting ecommerce. I think that the exposure that Web-based security breaches receive just adds to the mountain of distrust that already exists. However, the economic advantages of online commerce make it inevitable that companies will push harder for more customers to conduct business over this medium. At some point, there may be no other option. Also time is on the side of the Web. As the first generation of people who've grown up in the Information Age reach their majority, this distrust will diminish. However, strong security practices by individuals and companies, as well as software developers, must become commonplace.

But that is looking back. The question remains: Have we gotten ahead of the cybercrime curve? Will we ever?

Top Ten Trends Impacting Security

TREND 1: *The 'Evernet':* Billions of devices proliferate that are always on and always connected

TREND 2: *Virtual Business:* Complex outsourcing relationships extend trust boundaries beyond recognition

TREND 3: *Rules of Government:* Government regulation increases as lawmakers react to real losses that hurt

TREND 4: *Wild, Wild West:* International criminals exploit lack of cooperation and compatibility in international laws

TREND 5: *No More Secrets:* Privacy concerns will continue to compete with convenience and desire for features

TREND 6: *Haste Makes Waste:* 'Time to Market' increases pressure to sacrifice security and quality of software

TREND 7: *Talent Wars:* Lack of security skills will compound weaknesses of delivered solutions

TREND 8: *Yours, Mine or Ours:* Identifying intellectual property and information ownership will become key areas of debate

TREND 9: *Web of Trust:* Standard security architectures and improved trust will spur eCommerce growth

TREND 10: *Information Pollution:* Information exploitation becomes more lucrative than hacking.

Cybercrime Will Become More 'Normal'

I mentioned in a previous chapter how cybercrime is quickly losing its specialty status. In most important ways it is becoming like other crime. The best way to fight crime is to keep it from occurring. Any and all activity which can dissuade someone from committing a crime is time and money well spent. However, in most cases the only thing that law enforcement can do is allocate available resources to react to a crime. The only thing possible to do is to try and anticipate what a criminal will do, which is pretty damn difficult.

So where will cybercrime go from here? First and foremost it will be something that's just as common as burglaries and car thefts and other standard criminal actions. It will just be a natural part of police training. Just like investigators can now do paint transfers off of cars, they will soon all be able to identify where an email came from and other basic computer forensics. Consequently, we will have a cadre of people prepared to deal with cybercrime just as we now have law enforcement units devoted to types of crime, such as homicides and drugs and illegal immigration.

Identity Theft Will Provide the Most Challenges

Contemplating the future of threats is always an interesting endeavor. Unfortunately, as soon as we forecast we are wrong. We can do our best to anticipate what people will try to do next to get rich illegally. I expect that as we get better at software security, at identifying a tax on systems caused by outside intrusions, at reducing the likelihood of con games and social engineering through education and awareness and just through the growing maturity of users, we will actually start to see a growing trend toward impersonation and a real need to implement sophisticated identity management. In essence, the problem has migrated from protecting the systems. We have, to a large degree, gotten the idea and are now doing a pretty good job of protecting the devices, and this security will only get better. The more vulnerable part of the total system is now the person sitting behind the keyboard.

Since it will become more difficult to grab someone's property or to trick them out of it, criminals will need to resort to actually assuming the users' identity so they can take this property "legitimately." There is currently a concerted effort to build effective online digital identity security. Unfortunately, it is still probably five to 10 years before we have a strong national system based on passports and/or driver licenses or other controlled certifications that establish identification.

Building the infrastructure to accept and manage a type of higher level credential is a complex task. The whole futuristic concept of a digital identity begs the question: How do we know just who we are dealing with in the online world? IDs and passwords will no longer be sufficient. An individual's digital identity now has at least three components. There is a public persona for all to see, a private persona used for government and financial transactions, and there is an anonymous persona to be used to access the Internet without broadly declaring an identity. This requires the construction of an entirely new identity function. This is a really interesting, though incredibly difficult task that will probably not be bullet-proof.

While anonymity can be cool when surfing certain areas of the 'net, it is certainly not appropriate when interacting with bank or securities accounts. Providing a reasonable security perimeter around an individual's various identities to halt the common criminal element is essential for the Internet to reach the next level of utility. That level is based on trust.

The Disruptive Power of Distrust— Who are the Good Guys?

I went through the FBI's anti-terrorism school when I was on a SWAT team some years ago. One of the things that we discussed was the different psychological states, such as manic depression and schizophrenia, and how to handle people in these mental states during a hostage situation. The bottom line: Law enforcement never comes in shooting except when every other option has failed, and maybe not even then. One of the high-end objectives of terrorism is to get people to change the way that they do things and to become wary of things that they normally trust. Terrorists would love to foster the belief among a segment of the population that SWAT teams and other law enforcement always shoot first and then let God sort it out.

Taking an example from popular culture, there was this action-packed B movie featuring Chuck Norris called *Invasion USA*. It is very much a shoot 'em up and not everyone's cup of tea, but it provided an interesting and somewhat scary scenario. In the beginning of this movie some bad guys come up from South America and dress up like police. They then go into a bar within a Spanish barrio, start an altercation and begin shooting people. They don't act like cops. Cops ask questions and arrest people. They rarely fire their weapons and they don't just open fire and start killing people. In this movie, after this shooting occurs, the real police show up. Then people do not believe they are the real police and start shooting at them. A recipe for complete anarchy.

The analogy to ecommerce: You need to constantly trust the person you are doing business with. In a medium as cold as the Internet, trust is the most precious of commodities. It is also the most precarious. If cybercriminals can erode this structure of trust by stealing identities, the system will no longer be effective.

Reason for Optimism

Every year seems to bring a new target of opportunity to the cybercriminal. While it has at times been a battle that has been straight uphill, I have a tremendous amount of optimism that we will be able to apply a combination of tech-

> "That which we persist in doing becomes easier, not that the task itself has become easier, but that our ability to perform it has improved."
> **Ralph Waldo Emerson**

nology, policies and security best practices to bring and keep this problem under control. Stop it completely? Probably not. But keep it marginalized and not let it inhibit the use of the Internet in daily activities? Definitely!

I gave a keynote at the first-ever security conference in Singapore in 2005. Some 600-plus security response team people were there representing many different countries, businesses and universities. I outlined the progress we've already made. First, at that time it had been years since we'd had a significant worm or Trojan breakout. Sure, a few viruses and worms were significant enough to make TV news lineups, but they were basically isolated events. They may have impacted some specific organizations, but the rest of the world went on with their business. Even efforts to create large-scale bot networks have not been as successful as the bad guys hoped due to the successes of international law enforcement, private sector security experts and Internet service providers. Together we've closed down a number of botnets and identified various tools and technologies to combat this recent threat against IT systems.

Research done by Wenke Lee of Georgia Tech's Information Security Center has been extremely helpful in identifying bot networks in order that they be found and closed down.

After I finished talking, one of the guys in the audience said that's all well and good, but the fact is that we are not getting better, we have just been lucky that something bad hasn't happened and that all the people in this audience would agree with him instead of me. I thought about that comment for a minute (or longer) and replied that he was entitled to his opinion. However, what he was saying was that all the efforts of the people in the audience who'd put in all of those late nights updating signatures, updating security patches, writing tighter code to prevent a major outbreak were just spinning wheels.

I beg to differ.

The fact that security officers are now C-level executives has raised the visibility of security to where corporate-wide action can be implemented. Companies are training more people as Certified Information Systems Auditors (CISAs) and Certified Information Systems Security Professionals (CISSPs), which has certainly made a difference.

We have gotten better. We are constantly talking about security and discussing different methods to enhance it. We are implementing new and more effective policies. There are many things now being done that have never been done before. We now have a regimen on how to fix security patches. Most importantly, we now have response mechanisms in place.

When something happens it is no longer a decision of who to call. We know we are going to call a specific person or organization if it is one type of problem and another person or organization if it's a different situation. We are also confidant that who we call will have the expertise to deal with the problem. We also know that sometimes, we just have to pull the plug to prevent ourselves from spreading problems, and people are more willing to do so. When they do, they can still run things internally and safely until the problem is mitigated. This will disrupt things, but it will prevent the opportunity for a total systems meltdown.

Technology also has an important role. Somebody said to me once that they thought it wrong for security companies to build security products as a profit-making activity. These should be developed specifically for the common good. I have a fundamental problem with that. If we've got a problem that needs to be solved and somebody develops a solution to fix that problem and improves security they should make a profit off of it. That is the way a free market works. We basically have a problem, somebody comes up with an innovative way to fix it, the problem is fixed, it creates jobs and people make money off the deal. What's wrong with that? More security companies should be looking at how to inoculate the Web instead of waiting to benefit from fighting an existing problem.

We continue to develop a culture of security in the way we run IT systems. The more we try, the more we will succeed. All of this is reason to believe the bad guys can be kept at bay and we, as a society increasingly dependent on the virtual world, can thrive. We all need to do our part to secure our place in cyberspace.